Life FOUNDATIONS

Harrison House

Shippensburg, PA

Life FOUNDATIONS

SIX PILLARS
TO KNOWING
GOD, YOURSELF,
& IMPACTING
OTHERS

MIKE & CARRIE PICKETT

Dedication

To our amazing children Elliana and Michael. These are the Life Foundations we are committed to raise you in so you can have a powerful relationship with Jesus! You are both going to change the world!

Acknowledgments

To Andrew Wommack for the years of mentorship and foundations you have laid in our hearts and for the continued opportunity to help reach the world with the good news.

To our team and graduates we had in Russia, and for the thousands that have gone through this course. Watching you walk in the revelation of these Life Foundations has been inspiring. Thank you for letting us share these truths with you.

Published by Harrison House Publishers
Shippensburg, PA 17257

Cover design by Eileen Rockwell

ISBN 13 TP: 978-1-6803-1556-1

ISBN 13 eBook: 978-1-6803-1557-8

ISBN 13 HC: 978-1-6803-1559-2

ISBN 13 LP: 978-1-6803-1558-5

For Worldwide Distribution, Printed in the U.S.A.

3 4 5 6 7 8 / 25 24 23

Contents

LIFE FOUNDATION: THE TRUE NATURE OF GOD

LIFE FOUNDATION: BELIEVER'S AUTHORITY

APPENDIX

Foreword

Mike and Carrie Pickett have packed more ministry into the last twenty-two years than most people in a lifetime. After leaving Bible College, Carrie moved to the Soviet Union and lived north of the Arctic Circle in Murmansk, Russia, and planted our first overseas Bible College. She literally went on faith with very little support—and the Lord proved Himself faithful.

She moved the Bible school to St. Petersburg, continued ministry, and met her husband Mike, who was also serving as a missionary. Together they ran our Charis Bible College and AWM office in Russia for sixteen years. They translated and put our Gospel Truth program on TV across eleven time zones in Russia and throughout the Russian-speaking world. They oversaw the translation of twenty-two of my books and trained students from twenty-six different nations. Many of their graduates are now directing Bible schools and ministries in other nations.

During the last six years they have been back in Colorado working in Charis Bible College and are now directing the whole Charis system. They oversee seventeen foreign AWM offices and fifty schools.

Their oversight has taken them all around the world, and they have proven themselves well equipped and faithful in dealing with many challenging situations.

As they clearly explain in this book, our foundation is what everything else is built upon. They truly have built their lives, marriage, family, and ministry on the solid foundation of Jesus Christ and it shows in all they do. They are overseeing the training of more than 5,000 Charis students at any given time with thousands more who are the fruit of previous years. Their impact is already great, and they are just getting started.

I believe the truths they share in a conversational manner in this book will enlighten and equip you to make the main thing, the main thing. The Christian life isn't a sprint, it's a marathon. Anyone can start a marathon, but not everyone can finish. You will touch many more lives in a long, fruitful ministry than if you burn out after a few years as so many do. Also, the destination is not the only goal. We need to enjoy the journey.

I recommend Mike and Carrie as a couple and their ministry as one that I've observed for a very long time. They minister with a maturity that few possess at their age—and everything I see says that this is the Lord's doing and it's marvelous in our eyes (Psalm 118:23). They are doing this right and they will help you put your life on the firm foundation of Jesus Christ.

Do you want to not only start well but finish well? That doesn't happen accidentally. It takes a strategy, perseverance, time, and most importantly, a dynamic relationship with Jesus through the Holy Spirit. These life lessons Mike and Carrie have learned will help you on your journey. As they share their heart with you, I believe the Lord will work these same graces in your life and ministry.

—Andrew Wommack
President and Founder
Andrew Wommack Ministries and Charis Bible College

Introduction

Any engineer will tell you that the most important part of a structure is its foundation. An insufficient foundation limits a building's size and dictates that building's functionality. Without a solid foundation, buildings become unstable. They are subjected to the effects of wind, rain, and gravity. When engineering your life, an insufficient life foundation is just as debilitating.

In more than twenty years of ministry, Carrie and I have discovered that most people's problems are a result of a faulty foundation. They don't understand how much God loves them. They don't really know who they are in Christ or how God sees them. They wrap up their identity in what they do, instead of what Jesus has done for them. They misunderstand God's true nature and their spiritual authority; and as a result, their lives and ministries crack under pressure. Their relationship with God grows stagnant. They feel powerless to resist the enemy, or even recognize his attacks. And they believe themselves incapable of ministering to others.

If you've ever felt trapped by circumstances, ineffective in ministry, or just plain stuck in your relationship with God, this book is for you. The six points we share lay the foundation every believer needs in order to experience God's best. These principles—though simple in theory—will revolutionize your life when you put them into practice. They are the essential truths of God's Word, the building blocks of our salvation. First Corinthians says:

> For we are...God's building. According to the grace of God which was given to me, as a wise master builder I have laid the foundation, and another builds on it. But let each one take heed how he builds on it. For no other foundation can anyone lay than that which is laid, which is Jesus Christ (1 Corinthians 3:9-11).

We are God's building. Our foundation is Christ. And while that foundation cannot be improved upon, we must constantly attend to it. Psalm 11:3 says, *"If the foundations are destroyed, what can the righteous do?"* In other words, what hope is there? How can the righteous experience the abundant life Jesus came to provide if they allow their spiritual foundation to erode? (see John 10:10). Just like a building inspector would never approve a construction or remodeling project without first reviewing the building's foundation,, neither should we attempt to build our lives or ministries on anything other than Christ.

We pray, as the apostle Paul wrote, that as you read this book, the Holy Spirit would open the eyes of your understanding to know the *"hope of His calling,"* the richness of our inheritance, and *"the exceeding greatness of His power toward us who believe"* (Ephesians 1:18-19). That the power He worked in Christ would be demonstrated by us,

"His body, the fullness of Him," (Ephesians 1:23) as we build our lives on that firm spiritual foundation.

Life FOUNDATION

THE LOVE OF GOD

The Lord has appeared of old to me, saying: "Yes, I have loved you with an everlasting love; therefore with lovingkindness I have drawn you" (Jeremiah 31:3).

1

Rediscovering Our Foundation

The principles Carrie and I share in this book are the basic principles of relationship with God. They're the same principles the Lord used to radically transform our lives and build our marriage, family life, and ministry. They truly are life foundations.

Throughout this book, you will discover the true nature of God, explore your spiritual makeup, and learn how to see yourself as God sees you so you can walk in your spiritual authority. We ask that you examine your heart as you read. Reflect on God's character and consider each principle's application. Allow God to show you where faulty foundations have hindered your relationship with Him.

As you read our stories and peek into the things God has taught us, we pray your faith is made strong, that you begin to see yourself the way God sees you, and experience His love in a deeper way so you can live your life as a "little Christ" walking in your God-given authority.

First Timothy 6:6 says, *"godliness with contentment is great gain."* But that doesn't mean we are content with whatever life throws at us. *Contentment* does mean satisfaction, but *godliness* implies growth.

This verse means we find satisfaction in our relationship with God; we enjoy discovering the realities of who we are in Christ. We don't allow our flesh to limit who God created us to be.

As Christians, our lives should be more than a list of personal accomplishments. They should be testimonies of God's grace. Author and speaker Ryan Haley said you and I must "live a life that demands a supernatural explanation." Our lives should be so full of God's love and power that the world takes note as the disciples did when *"they realized that they had been with Jesus"* (Acts 4:13). But to do that, we must rediscover our foundation.

In many ways, my and Carrie's stories mirror one another. We both grew up in church. We both served on the mission fields of Russia. We both had a zeal and hunger for God's Word. But it wasn't until after we married that I began to realize just how different our relationships with God were. Carrie's relationship was built on a foundation of God's love and character. Mine was built on family tradition.

Though I was a Christian for more than twenty years when Carrie and I met, I thought the Christian life was about *my work for God—* not *His work in me.* I thought God could only love me in proportion to my righteousness. That the way He saw me was dependent on how well I performed. I knew God was holy, but I was also abundantly aware of my own shortcomings. I believed my sin was a constant hindrance to relationship with God. When I did the right thing, I was confident approaching Him in prayer. When I did something stupid, I felt I had no right to ask anything of God. And though I knew, theoretically, that Jesus' sacrifice took care of sin, I hadn't discovered what that meant personally.

Carrie's relationship with God didn't fluctuate like mine. She knew God loved her. She knew God heard her prayers and that He delighted in answering them—regardless of how well she performed Christian rituals. I believed God *could* answer prayer. Carrie believed He longed to show Himself strong on her behalf (2 Chronicles 16:9).

The first time I heard Andrew Wommack speak, it rocked my world. God literally shook my foundation. Nearly everything Andrew said went against what I believed about God, but he proved it all with Scripture! I knew I couldn't argue with the Bible, God's Word, so as Andrew preached, I made note of all the questions his teaching raised. As God answered each question, I realized how wrong I'd been.

For twenty-two years of my life, I'd misjudged God. Everything I had done for Him was actually done in self-service. I didn't attend church, tithe, or help others because I had a real relationship with God—I served to make myself feel better. I realized I had tried to build my life on an unstable foundation. So for the next several years, God systematically took me back through the elementary principles of His Word. He shook loose all man-made tradition so I could rebuild my life on His truth.

As God was taking Mike through this process, He was working on me too. I grew up listening to solid, full-gospel teaching. I knew the basic principles of God's Word. I was even teaching them at Charis Bible College, Andrew Wommack's Bible school! But that was the problem. I *knew* them.

I remember standing at the kitchen sink one day while Mike was listening to Andrew's teachings in the other room. We'd only been married a couple of weeks, so I wasn't used to having someone else in my Russian apartment. When I heard someone shout, I rushed out of the kitchen with knife in hand. This country girl was ready for battle! It took me a second to realize it was just Mike. He was so excited about the things he was hearing from Andrew, he started shouting. By the time I got there, he was rambling, "Andrew just said... Did you know that? I mean it's right here in the Word...I've just never seen it before!"

And in that moment, the Holy Spirit pricked my heart. I did know the principles Mike was discovering, but I'd lost his sense of awe. I'd become complacent. I knew God loved me. I knew I was righteous. I knew grace gave me the power to get back up when I failed so I could keep moving forward. But I had moved beyond those elementary truths to "more spiritual" ones. I'd stopped valuing my foundation. As director of the Bible school in Saint Petersburg, Russia, I'd even started assigning new, inexperienced teachers to the first-year courses. I thought of that material as the easy stuff.

But as I watched Mike discover his spiritual foundation in Christ, I began rediscovering mine. I realized that all the other biblical truths and applications of the Word—healing, leadership dynamics, effective preaching strategies, everything else—were built on the foundation of the gospel. God showed me that though the gospel message was simple, I could spend the entirety of my life plumbing its depths and still never reach the bottom. My husband's growth process lit a fire in me, a passion to return to my foundation.

God is calling each of us to return to our foundations. Too often we think we need something new—a revelation beyond the gospel—to keep growing in relationship with Him. But there's nothing more spiritual than the gospel. God wants us to know Him. He wants us to understand His ways and walk in His truth. That's why, throughout history, God has kept His dealings with us humans simple. Unfortunately, humankind has a tendency to overlook the simplicity of the gospel. We complicate His Word with tradition and let fine-sounding arguments sway our opinions. But if we simply returned to the foundations of God's wisdom in the Bible—to the simplicity of the gospel—His Word will empower the transformation of our heart and mind and character. A transformation that would impact the world.

Transformation happens through the knowledge and application of God's Word. One of the most profound things anyone ever said to me is, "You don't know what you don't know." It's true. The Word of God is full of things we don't yet know. But as kings and priests of God, we have the awesome privilege of searching those things out (Proverbs 25:2). Part of the transformation process God is calling us to, is laying down our right to ourselves, and taking up our right to be like Jesus. Romans 8:28-30 (NLT) says:

And we know that God causes everything to work together for the good of those who love God and are called according to his purpose for them. For God knew his people in advance, and he chose them to become like his Son, so that his Son would be the firstborn among many brothers and sisters. And having chosen them, he called them to come to him. And having called them, he gave them right standing with himself. And having given them right standing, he gave them his glory.

Many believers misunderstand this passage of Scripture. While it's true that God works all things together for our good, that does not mean everything that has happened in life is good. Nor does it mean everything was God-ordained. What this Scripture does tell us is that God is an expert at taking the ash of our lives and making something beautiful from it (Isaiah 61:3). He can take what the enemy meant for evil, touch it with His power, and cause it to be a blessing to others, a source of irritation to the devil, and to ultimately bring Him glory.

When God looks at us, He does not see our faults and failures. He does not see our scars. He sees opportunity—opportunity for another beloved child to become like His Son. But God does not ask us to make this change on our own. He graciously calls us to Himself in Christ. By faith, He gives us right standing with Him, then invites us into an intimate relationship with Him in which we also share in His glory.

So, faith is a continual walk with God, not a Sunday club. It is relationship with God—relationship while at home with your children, relationship while driving to work, relationship in the morning and at night lying in bed. It's learning to abide in Jesus and allowing His Word to abide in you to the point that it's no longer your life. It's His life lived through you (Galatians 2:20). This means the foundational truths of God's Word cannot be truths we hear once and then outgrow. They must become part of our daily lives.

Not allowing the Word to abide in us makes us easy targets of the enemy. Our enemy, the devil, is constantly looking for someone to devour, someone to "outgrow" the truths of God's Word and believe his lies (1 Peter 5:8). The devil is waiting for our focus to shift off what God has done, to what we can do to earn God's love and acceptance.

Too often religion convinces people that their works, sin, and failure are direct reflections of who they are. Religion causes people to believe that the road to redemption is too long or the rules too hard. And they lose hope. Others fear the abuse or sickness they've experienced in life has warped their destiny. They crave freedom, but believe tragedy and struggle will always color their interactions with God and others. That is not an accurate reflection of relationship with God!

God is calling us to return to the basic principles of His Word— not a set of rules. No one has too far to go for God to love. No one has too much to learn for God to use or bless. We simply need to rest in the finished work of Christ and learn to build our lives on *that* foundation.

Years ago, as we were teaching these things, a woman approached us. She was probably in her mid-sixties when we chatted and had been a Christian her whole life, but she simply couldn't wrap her mind around God's love and grace. All her life she had heard that "God loved her when..." and "If she loved God, she'd..." She had never heard anyone say that God simply wanted relationship with her. She told us that as she wrestled with this concept, she asked the Lord, "Why can't I receive this?"

He replied, "Because your receiver is broken."

That was such an important revelation to her and to us.

Many of us are professional "doers." We strive to prove our love for God through ministry and service, forgetting—like Martha—the most important thing (Luke 10:38-42). But God calls each of us to be a receiver before He ever asks us to be a doer. Imagine a television. How does it broadcast your favorite shows? Does it produce pictures of itself? Are there little people with terrible accents pretending to be astronauts and racecar drivers in your television set? Of course not! A television is simply a receiver. It receives whatever the networks decide to broadcast and displays that show.

That's exactly what you and I are called to be—receivers. First John 4:19 says, *"We love Him because He first loved us."* As Christians, we are called to be God's receivers, to attach our lives to Him and simply display His goodness. God never asks us to figure it out; He doesn't expect us to save anyone or be their healer. He knows we cannot love before we are first loved. We cannot give what we do not have. God simply asks us to tune our lives to His frequency and allow His life to flow through us. He asks us to receive.

As we dive into *Life Foundations* together, let us determine to keep these principles in their proper place. May they never become burdensome or part of our spiritual "to-do" lists. Instead, allow them to revitalize and revolutionize our walk with God. We're all at different places in relationship with God. Perhaps you've only recently been saved or filled with the Spirit. Maybe you just graduated Bible college or answered a call to ministry. Celebrate those milestones! But don't assume any certificate you receive is a diploma. Think of it as a birth certificate—an acknowledgment of your decision to take another step in this amazing walk of faith. Keep learning, keep receiving, and keep discovering the awesome foundation you've been given!

2

A Covenantal Relationship

The single most important revelation we can have as believers is the revelation of God's love. Love answers the foundational questions of our hearts, including: Why am I here? Why would God choose me? How could He forgive me? Why would He exchange His Son's life for mine?

Unfortunately, the answer to those questions—because God loves you—is often misrepresented in religious circles.

Religion weakens God's love by comparing it to human love. Religion says God's love is indifferent. It is fleeting and emotional. It is easily offended and not entirely trustworthy. But that's not what the Bible says about God's kind of love. God's love lasts; it is not like conditional, short-lived human love. God's love does not fluctuate. Jeremiah 31:3 says God appeared to him and said, *"...I have loved you with an everlasting love; therefore with lovingkindness I have drawn you."*

God's love cannot be earned. It is an unconditional love. He does not love you for what you can do for Him. Nor does He stop loving you because you forgot to read your Bible or didn't participate in the all-church outreach program. God's love is not based on your past failures or successes:

> *...the love of God has been poured out in our hearts by the Holy Spirit who was given to us. For...God demonstrates His own love toward us, in that **while we were still sinners**, Christ died for us* (Romans 5:5,8).

God's love is based on His character (1 John 4:16). John, one of Jesus' disciples and closest friends, understood God's love like no other. He taught that God's kind of love is a sacrificial choice expressing itself through action.

> *For God so loved the world that He **gave** His only begotten Son, that whoever believes in Him should not perish but have everlasting life. For God did not send His Son into the world to condemn the world, but that the world through Him might be saved* (John 3:16-17).

If you've been in church any length of time, I'm sure you can quote this passage of Scripture. But we must be careful not let its familiarity steal its power. Notice to whom God directed His love. God didn't just love the Jew. He didn't only love those worthy of His love. John says that God loved the entire world—a world worthy of condemnation. And because God loved the world, He *"gave."* He gave the best He had to give. He gave Himself.

Whether or not we realize it, each of us carries around an internal picture of love. And for the majority of us, it's wrong. Our ideas of love have been distorted by experience and warped by what we see in movies or read in books. As a result, we view God's kind of love as contractual. A contract is a document that governs a mutually beneficial exchange. In a contract, one party agrees to sell a product or perform a service *in exchange* for money or another service. Should one party make a mistake or miss a deadline, the contract becomes void and the other is free to walk away without penalty. They are no longer bound by their agreement. But God does not view relationship in that way.

> *Know therefore that the Lord your God is God; he is the faithful God, keeping his covenant of love to a thousand generations of those who love him and keep his commandments* (Deuteronomy 7:9 NIV).

God does not make contracts. He makes *covenants.* Relationship with God is not a "mutually beneficial exchange." He does not love us when we prove our love to Him. He offers relationship based on a covenant of love expressed through action. When God saw creation in an impossible situation—helplessly bound by sin—He stepped forward to do what we couldn't. Love made a way to come to us in covenant. Through the cross of Christ, God's love utterly destroyed what kept us separated from Himself. And this, John says, is how we know what true love is—Jesus laid down His life for us.

> *By this we know love, because He laid down His life for us. And we also ought to lay down our lives for the brethren* (1 John 3:16).

Before God shook my foundations and brought me back to the simplicity of the gospel, I struggled with this concept. I couldn't understand how a holy God could love me even when I failed. I questioned how God could overlook my stupid choices. How my mistakes didn't motivate God to distance Himself from me—even though they motivated others in my life to do so.

Then in my season of receiving, I heard Andrew Wommack say Jesus would be the only Person in Heaven with scars. That struck me. The Creator of the universe willingly stepped off His throne to rescue me. He laid down His life and suffered as no one has ever suffered to prove the height and depth and breadth of His love (John 15:13). Jesus fulfilled the "contractual obligations" of the law and opened the way for true covenantal relationship with God. And all that He suffered on my behalf—in a commitment to demonstrate His love—will be with Him for eternity. He will never forget His love for me. He will always carry the scars. That's amazing!

Everything God does is motivated by love. Understanding this gives us the faith we need to run to Him in all of life's circumstances. Our lives do not have to be a roller coaster of good and bad days. God's love trumps everything. It is greater than our past, greater than any doctor's report or repair bill. His love is greater than the future. And because of that, we can trust Him.

When we make mistakes or endure hardship, we don't have to question God's love. Second Timothy 2:13 says, *"If we are faithless, He remains faithful; He cannot deny Himself."* That means no matter what we do or don't do, God's covenant of love will not change. Jesus made us accepted in the beloved.

Blessed be the God and Father of our Lord Jesus Christ, who has blessed us with every spiritual blessing in the heavenly places in Christ, just as He chose us in Him before the foundation of the world, that we should be holy and without blame before Him in love, having predestined us to adoption as sons by Jesus Christ to Himself, according to the good pleasure of His will, to the praise of the glory of His grace, by which He made us accepted in the Beloved (Ephesians 1:3-6).

God doesn't love us because we are lovely. He loves us because that's who He is. Though First John 4:8 says *"God is love,"* many believers have a hard time accepting that truth. Because we've been trained to find and fix our flaws and imperfections, we think God looks for them too. Consider what we do each time we look in a mirror. We never look for the good. We look for the things out of place. We look for the pimples and flyaway hairs. We look for that piece of broccoli stuck in our teeth. God doesn't do that. He doesn't search out our imperfections. He covers them with His love (1 Peter 4:8).

Though the world says, "I love you when...I love you if...I love you because," God says, "I love you—period." The apostle Paul considered this revelation to be the foundation of every believer's life in Christ:

I pray that out of his glorious riches he may strengthen you with power through his Spirit in your inner being, so that Christ may dwell in your hearts through faith. And I pray that you, being rooted and established in love, may have power, together with all the Lord's holy

people, to grasp how wide and long and high and deep
is the love of Christ, and to know this love that surpasses
knowledge—that you may be filled to the measure of all
the fullness of God (Ephesians 3:16-19 NIV).

God wants to rewrite your definition of love. He wants to stir up your childlike faith and give you a hope for the future. But you have to learn to let God love you. When the past is colored by hurt and disappointment, it's easy to put up barriers to protect yourself from more hurt. But don't put up those barriers with God. Don't hold Him at a distance. He is the only One who can truly heal your hurts.

I read a book by Richard Wurmbrand, a Romanian pastor who was beaten and tortured for his faith. For fourteen years, communists imprisoned Wurmbrand, giving him just enough food and water to stay alive. When he was finally released, scars covered his body. People couldn't understand how he survived. Wurmbrand said God's love sustained him. In prison, he couldn't remember Scripture, but he remembered the song, "Jesus loves me this I know...." So he held on to that.

If you're struggling to trust God or believe His promises, if you're struggling with fear, you don't have a faith problem—you have a love problem. You don't yet know how much God loves you. First John 4:18 says, *"There is no fear in love; but perfect love casts out fear, because fear involves torment. But he who fears has not been made perfect in love."* Love conquerors fear. It gives us confidence and releases God's power in our lives.

Instead of running from our issues, love gives us the strength to stand and fight. Open your heart to God's love. Know that He has a good plan for your life. His thoughts toward you are peace (Jeremiah 29:11). He rejoices over you with singing (Zephaniah 3:17). Don't fall into the trap of earning God's love or favor. Don't superimpose your experience of human "love" onto your expectations of God's love. Receive His love for you and let His love motivate you to respond in faith (1 John 4:9-10).

Once while teaching these things to a group of pastors in the Congo, a man stood up and said, "For years I taught the love of God exclusively. Then someone told me I couldn't be very spiritual to teach such a simple message. So I stopped teaching God's love and started working on creating deep theological messages to prove how spiritual I was. Now I understand *love* is the most important thing for me to teach."

How true! Beloved, when life gets hard and the enemy attacks, he doesn't come bashing our knowledge of Greek and Hebrew. He comes to make us question God's love. He says things like, "If God really loved you, this wouldn't have happened. How can you trust a God who is good one day and not the next? There's no way God could love you now. How can you please a God whose standard is that unattainable?"

That's why it's so important for us to know the Word and to be *"looking unto Jesus, the author and finisher of our faith..."* (Hebrews 12:2). Jesus came to demonstrate the Father's love and invite us into a covenantal relationship with Him—a relationship *not* based on our performance.

Jesus said to him, "I am the way, the truth, and the life. No one comes to the Father except through Me. If you had known Me, you would have known My Father also; and from now on you know Him and have seen Him." Philip said to Him, "Lord, show us the Father, and it is sufficient for us." Jesus said to him, "Have I been with you so long, and yet you have not known Me, Philip? He who has seen Me has seen the Father..." (John 14:6-9).

Jesus demonstrated a side of God's character, through the gospel, the Jewish people had forgotten. Though they had experienced His mercy and love throughout the Old Testament, God's people stubbornly held to their sin and repeatedly abandoned relationship with Him. Then God finally sent this message through the prophet Amos: *"'Behold, the days are coming,' says the Lord God, 'That I will send a famine on the land, not a famine of bread, nor a thirst for water, but of hearing the words of the Lord'"* (Amos 8:11)—and for nearly 400 years, the heavens fell silent.

But as the people returned to God's Word, what they saw warped their understanding of Him. In the Law, they saw a god who was hard to please, a wrathful god who exacted vengeance (Exodus 20:5). They missed the gracious God their books of history, poetry, and prophecy revealed. They missed the God who was slow to anger and abounding in love and forgiveness (Psalm 86:15). So when Jesus appeared preaching the Kingdom and *"healing all who were oppressed of the devil,"* the Jews did not recognize Him (Acts 10:38 and 13:27). They were not looking for a God *"moved with compassion"* (Matthew 9:36). They were looking for a conquering king.

Jesus didn't fit the Jews' preconceived notions of God. Unlike their religious leaders, Jesus didn't pity the people; He had compassion on them. Pity suggests condemnation. Jesus didn't come to Earth saying, "Oh, these poor people...look what their choices have brought them to." But neither was He merely sympathetic of our plight. He didn't maintain distance like the priest who wouldn't help the man fallen among thieves (Luke 10:25-37). Jesus stepped into our struggle. He became a man, experienced our pain, and was tempted as we are (Hebrews 4:15).

Compassion is God's love in action. Each time the Scriptures say Jesus was *"moved with compassion,"* miracles followed. The lame walked. The sick were healed. The blind received their sight. And we—both Jew and Gentile alike—were brought into fellowship with God. Now, the more we allow God's love to change our hearts and minds, the more we will experience His Kingdom.

3

Understanding God's Love

As believers, we must become aware of the fact that the whole of the Christian life is this dynamic of God's love creating movement toward us. That's the difference between true relationship with God and religion. Religion says you have to take steps toward God before He can love you. But the Bible says that our movement toward God is secondary. We love Him *"because He first loved us"* (1 John 4:19). God is the great Initiator. He is the Husbandman. He woos us to Himself; and even after we are saved, His love continues to pursue us—making movement toward our finances, movement toward our health, movement that brings us joy and peace.

God's love changed the way I saw His Word, the Bible. For twenty-two years, I read the Word and saw law. I saw God's commands as limitations on my life. I saw His discipline as punishment for my behavior. I didn't understand *why* He did and said the things He did. But when I began to understand His love, my perspective changed. I began to see His commands as protection, His discipline as correction. Every time I read the Word now, I discover another verse about God's love.

While we were in Russia, the Lord spoke to our hearts about focusing our teaching on His love. "Tell the people of Russia I love them," God said. "Tell them that I am not a communist God. I am not a dictator. I am not a father who abuses or abandons them. I am the God who loves them." So we began putting red hearts next to each verse that demonstrated His love. Now, we can hardly turn a page in either of our Bibles without seeing red! First John 4:8 tells us that *"God is love,"* but when we don't know what love is—what it looks like or how it behaves—neither do we know who God is, what He looks like, or how He behaves.

First Corinthians gives us this definition of love:

> *Love suffers long and is kind; love does not envy; love does not parade itself, is not puffed up; does not behave rudely, does not seek its own, is not provoked, thinks no evil; does not rejoice in iniquity, but rejoices in the truth; bears all things, believes all things, hopes all things, endures all things. Love never fails...* (1 Corinthians 13:4-8).

For many years, this passage of Scripture was my "to-love" list. In it were all the attributes I felt I needed to truly love someone— or evaluate their love for me. It wasn't until I began rebuilding my life on the foundational truths of God's Word that I realized that Paul was actually describing God's kind of love toward me. God's love toward me is patient and kind. His love never behaves rudely or becomes provoked. His love never devises evil to teach me a lesson, instead it rejoices when I understand the truth. God's love endured all things for my sake, and His love will never fail. That is the definition of love—the definition of God—and that is what His grace is built upon.

Everything God wants to do in your life comes from His nature of love. Years ago, Carrie and I introduced this concept to a group of pastors in Russia. We were teaching in a church called Della Vera (which means "Works of Faith") and discovered that the whole of their doctrine revolved around that idea. To them, Christianity was a life spent repaying God for all He had done to secure eternal salvation for them. As ministers, Carrie and I were trying to express God's love for and grace toward these pastors apart from their works, but it was like plowing rock. They just didn't get it. We kept saying things like, "God loves you. He wants relationship with you. He doesn't love you for what you can do for Him. He's not interested in the size of your church or the number of service projects you host each year. He loves *you*." We shared hundreds of Scriptures illustrating these points with them, but for three days our words fell like lead on their ears.

Eventually, the Word broke through that hardness of heart and we saw the revelation of God's love work amazing things in their lives, and over the course of time, in their churches. But that weekend taught us just how hard it is to receive grace—or see God's promises work in our lives—when we don't understand how much He loves us. Without love, *grace* is a foreign word.

Grace (which we will discuss in more detail later) is the unmerited favor and love of God. It is His influence and power in our lives, His working on our behalf. It is all the good things we receive from God independent of our worth or worthiness. In a nutshell, the grace of God is Jesus. Yet how many Christians say they have a revelation of Jesus—a revelation of God's love—but feel unworthy or unqualified to receive the rest of His blessings? They are deceived. You cannot truly understand God's love and think like that.

Romans 8:32 says, *"He who did not spare His own Son,"* speaking of God sacrificing Jesus on our behalf, *"but delivered Him up for us all, how shall He not with Him also freely give us all things?"* Too many people are satisfied with forgiveness. For them, "salvation" is about their eternal resting place and that is enough. If they have to deal with sickness or fear or poverty or depression between now and then, "at least they're on their way to heaven." We meet too many people who think they shouldn't ask God for more. "He's done enough," they say.

But forgiveness is just the first page of our love story with God! Salvation is more than forgiveness. It's more than just redemption from sin—though that is a wonderful benefit. Salvation is experiencing the *zoe* life of God—life that embraces wholeness in spirit, soul, and body. Salvation is real life. It's forgiveness, redemption, healing, peace, prosperity, sanctification, and so much more! True salvation is living in our inheritance of love.

Our spiritual inheritance is something many Christians misunderstand. They think of it as something they get after they die and go to Heaven. But no one gets an inheritance when they die! We receive an inheritance when Someone else died. Jesus died so that you and I could receive our spiritual inheritance right now. We don't have to wait for Heaven to know wisdom and peace. We don't have to wait for Heaven to experience healing. Walking the streets of gold is not the only place we can have prosperity (1 Corinthians 1:7). As wonderful as Heaven will be, it is only *part* of our spiritual inheritance in Christ. Let's look again at what Paul wrote to the Ephesian church:

I pray that out of his glorious riches he may strengthen you with power through his Spirit in your inner being, so that Christ may dwell in your hearts through faith. And I pray that you, being rooted and established in love, may have power, together with all the Lord's holy people, to grasp how wide and long and high and deep is the love of Christ, and to know this love that surpasses knowledge—that you may be filled to the measure of all the fullness of God (Ephesians 3:16-19 NIV).

According to Scripture, everything God has—His "fullness"—is our spiritual inheritance. A true revelation of that should birth within us a hunger to experience *all* His goodness, not just in the life to come, but in this life as well. It is not selfish to want to know God. It is not greed to desire to walk in the fullness of His promises. The writer of Psalm 84 says, *"For the Lord God is a sun and shield... no good thing will He withhold from those who walk uprightly"* (Psalm 84:11). Christ's death and resurrection enabled us to walk uprightly before God. So according to this verse we should expect that God will not withhold good from us.

What confidence the love of God brings! God's love allows us to approach Him for anything we need, not because of our righteousness, but because of His grace. We are God's children (Hebrews 4:16); and just like our children don't need permission to approach us, we don't need permission to approach God. If my son were to visit me at work, it wouldn't matter what meeting I was in or who I was talking to, nothing could keep him from me. He would boldly barge into my office shouting, "Hey, Dad!" He would fearlessly climb into my lap and hug my neck. He knows no matter what is going on I'll receive him.

The same is true when we walk into the throne room of God. We don't need to fear entering His presence. We don't need permission to approach Him. He is our Father (Hebrews 4:16). Nothing can come between us. No one can keep us apart. We don't need a special song or anointing to receive from Him. He is not withholding His love, His Spirit, or His blessings from us.

The Scriptures declare that God's love *"has been shed abroad in our hearts"* (Romans 5:5 KJV). But many Christians fail to see God's love personally. They know He loved the world enough to send His Son, but it's not enough to know God loved the world. We need to know He loves us.

It's not enough to know God rescued Daniel from the lion's den. We need to know He will rescue us. It's not enough to know Jesus healed the blind man. We need to know that Jesus offers that same healing to us. Jesus paid for our blindness and healing on the cross. He tasted death—and all that entails—so we could walk in newness of life (Romans 6:4). God did not love us just enough to offer redemption; He threw His love around like confetti! And like confetti, His love touches every part of our lives. God is not far away. He is not removed from our circumstance.

When the enemy whispers that our faith isn't working, we need to remind ourselves of God's love. We need to remind ourselves of all God provided for us in Christ. We need to start speaking God's love over our situations and relationships, over our hearts. Let Love remind us of First John 4:16, *"God is love,"* and First Corinthians 13:8, *"Love never fails,"* to the point it stirs up our faith. Because *"God is love"* and *"Love never fails,"* God never fails. His promises are true. They are declarations of His love toward us. We don't have to know the future or figure out where the money for new brakes is coming from. We know our life is in God's hands, and like a child, we can simply rest in our Father's love. Theologian and pastor John Piper said, "God is most glorified in us when we are most satisfied in God."

One of our favorite things to do is spend time with our children without agenda, plan, or schedule. It's in those moments when the wonder and beauty of life shines brightest. When our son comes to us with a new scientific discovery, we don't cringe or roll our eyes. We don't dismiss his excitement. When he says, "Mom, Dad, check out that cloud! Did you know the sky isn't really blue? It only looks that way because light scatters." We respond, "We know, buddy. Isn't creation amazing?"

God does that too. He loves being around His children. He doesn't cringe or roll His eyes when we pray. He doesn't dismiss our concerns or our excitement. He desires to meet our needs and spend time with us. It blesses God when we trust Him for our futures, when we come to Him with our questions. He loves hearing our ideas—even the stupid ones. He loves celebrating our discoveries. It's all part of developing a love-relationship with Him. Relationship takes time. It is a process. But it is how a solid life foundation begins.

When our daughter, Elliana, was young, we told her of Jesus' love by highlighting God's love toward her in everyday life. Whenever she received a birthday present or there was an answer to prayer, we'd say, "Look how much Jesus loves you!" Once while we were in Russia, Ellie saw a bunch of kids rollerblading. She wanted to join in but didn't have any rollerblades. "I want some," she told me pointing toward the group. And while I should have told her to ask God, all I said was, "Maybe someday you will."

Later that day, our interpreter came over to our home and said, "My daughter grew out of her rollerblades and I thought Ellie might like them." I couldn't believe it! She had just asked for rollerblades. I turned to Ellie and said, "Look how much Jesus loves you!"

Unfortunately, the rollerblades didn't fit, and Ellie was terribly disappointed. We tried to encourage her, but three-year-olds don't understand blessings that you have to wait for. Long story short, just before midnight our translator returned. "I felt so bad the skates didn't fit, I bought Elliana new ones." He had bought her a helmet and pads, too. What a blessing! When Ellie saw her gift, she didn't even say thank you. She just squealed and ran around in circles saying, "Look how much Jesus loves me!"

God wants to lavish His love on us like that. Not that we'll all get rollerblades, but there are issues in your life and questions in your heart that God wants to answer. He wants to show up and show off—not just in big miracles but through the little things as well.

Out on the plains where the sky is big and city lights are far away, falling stars seem almost magical. When I was growing up, every falling star was like a whisper from God saying, "I love you, Carrie."

I saw thousands of them until I moved to the smog-filled skies of St. Petersburg, Russia. One night while I was home visiting my family, my sister and I went out for a walk.

As we walked she said, "You know, I've never seen a falling star."

"Really? That's how God tells me He loves me," I responded.

"I want to see a falling star!"

"Okay," I said without thinking. "Let's find one." As we walked I prayed, *God, help! She needs to know You love her, but I can't make this happen.*

A few moments later, my sister gasped, "I just saw a falling star! God loves me!"

"He sure does!" I replied.

"I want to see how much He *really* loves me," she said. Thirty seconds later I heard her gasp again. This time as I looked to the sky, I saw a huge comet streak across it in flames of yellow, blue, and green. "Wow!" we both said. "God *really* loves me!"

Beloved, God loves you and He wants to express His love to you in a personal way. Let Him love you—even when it feels foolish or "unspiritual." Jesus told the disciples that unless they humbled themselves like a little child, they could not experience the Kingdom of God (Matthew 18:3). Let's believe God. Let's come to Him as a child and let Him lavish us with His love. Let's experience His Kingdom.

4

What Love Produces

In Matthew 22:34-36, a lawyer and member of the Pharisees came to Jesus with a question. This lawyer wanted to know Jesus' opinion, asking, *"Teacher, which is the greatest commandment in the law?"* Like all lawyers, this one spent hours a day analyzing every jot and tittle of the Mosaic Law, but his study didn't lead to Christ. It led to self-justification. (As Christians, we all have to guard against this same tendency. At one time, as a "lawman," I too struggled with the need to prove myself worthy of God's love, presence, and power.) Jesus told the lawyer:

> *"You shall love the Lord your God with all your heart, with all your soul, and with all your mind." This is the first and great commandment. And the second is like it: "You shall love your neighbor as yourself." On these two commandments hang all the Law and the Prophets* (Matthew 22:37-40).

Jesus responded to this lawyer in the context of his question, *"On these two commandments hang all the Law and the Prophets."* He responded according to the law. The fundamental constant of the law is performance. Performance in both how we treat others and how we measure up to God's standard of righteousness. It's not about grace. Yet, even under the law, Jesus said love—loving God and loving others—was the most important commandment. The difference for those of us under grace is that our debt to love has been paid. Jesus obeyed the law on our behalf (Matthew 5:17). He fulfilled the law so that the *obligation* to love is removed. Now grace empowers us to love God and others as Jesus did.

Love is a fruit of our relationship with God, the inspiration for everything we do. Love motivates us to respond to God in trust and obedience. It prompts us to abandon our comfort zone and fulfill God's will in the earth (Philippians 2:13; 1 John 4:11). When we know God loves us, we trust that He has only good for us. And when we trust His goodness, we respond by obeying His commands. We are able to surrender our lives joyfully, knowing that His plans are better. If God calls us to Russia, we obey knowing He would never ask us to do something that wasn't in our best interest. If He asks us to lay down a career to raise our family, we trust that He will be our provision.

Paul said *"the love of Christ compels us"* (2 Corinthians 5:14). It moves us to action. It shows the world we belong to Christ. John 13:35 says, *"By this all will know that you are My disciples, if you have love for one another."* Knowing how much God loves us helps us understand how much God loves our neighbors, our families, and our coworkers. If they are frustrating us or going through difficulties, we don't judge or condemn them. We don't worry. We love. We offer encouragement to the weary, hope to the hopeless, and grace to those who stumble.

Once, while a single woman in Russia, my family was going through some difficult circumstances at home. As the oldest of six kids, I felt responsible to help. I prayed, "Lord, what do I do?" And the Lord responded, "Stop worrying. I love them more than you do." That simple word was wisdom and revelation to me. In that moment, Love changed my perspective! I was able to let go of the worry to meet my family's needs and trust that God's love was working on their behalf. I never let go of my prayers or stopped speaking life over them, but I did stop trying to control their situations.

It's easy to get frustrated or offended when someone you're close to refuses to let go of immaturity, selfishness, and pride. But you can't let other people's attitudes ruin your life. People make dumb decisions. They can be malicious. They lie. They cheat. They do horrible things to get ahead. But no matter what's been said about or done to you, God's love does not change. So choose not to be offended.

I remember hearing a story about a Chinese pastor imprisoned for his faith. While in prison, one of the guards took particular delight in torturing this pastor. He would force the man to his knees and beat him until he was unconscious, all the while asking, "Where's your all-powerful God now?"

One day as he was being beaten, the pastor looked at his captor and said, "I have the power..." The guard became so furious he nearly beat the man to death. Twenty-four hours later, the guard dragged him out of his cell again and forced him to his knees. Again, the pastor said, "I have the power..."

"Really!" the guard shouted. "What power do you have?" he asked raising his fist to beat the man again.

"I have the power to love you," the pastor replied.

The guard staggered back and fell to his knees at those words. He felt God's presence. Seeing God's love in action affected him so deeply, he gave his heart to the Lord.

Beloved, God's love ruins us for offense. Dwelling on another's hurtful words or harmful actions is like drinking poison and expecting the other person to die from it. Jesus knew this. That's part of the reason John 2:24 says, *"But Jesus didn't trust them, because he knew all about people."* People are fickle. One day it's *"Hosanna!"* and the next *"Crucify Him!"* (John 12:13; 19:15). God's love is not like that. It never changes. It gives us stability and settles our emotions. God's love helps us maintain consistency in life.

After Mike and I were married, we took a cruise to the Caribbean islands. It was an awesome experience, but one night at dinner we ran into rough seas. The boat started rocking and my stomach started rolling. It was awful. As we made our way back to the cabin, Mike took me out on the balcony to watch the sun set. Though the seas were rough, it was a beautiful moment. And before long, with my eyes fixed on the horizon, my stomach settled. I stopped being led by the rocking of the boat. God's love is like that. It is a fixed point. No matter how hard the situations of life rock our emotions, if we keep our eyes fixed on His love, we will have peace (Isaiah 26:3). We will be guided by the steadfastness of His love and character, not by the wavering nature of our circumstances.

The best way to live the Christian life is through the lens of God's love. Understanding God's love changes our identity. It transforms our hearts so that others see Jesus in our nature, our character, and our service. They see Him in what we say yes to. They see Him in what we say no to. Love also changes the way we see ourselves. It changes the way we respond under pressure. We develop a scriptural attitude that because God loves me, it doesn't really matter what people do or say about me (Psalm 118:6). Because God loves me, how dare the enemy try to lie to, or steal from me (John 10:10). When used properly, this attitude of faith stirs up a righteous indignation in our hearts that helps us stand against the enemy's schemes. God's love sustains us in difficulty and empowers us to look beyond ourselves—like Jesus did—to the needs of others.

When our identity is caught up in human love, acceptance, and opinion, it restrains us. It keeps us from living life as God intended. Growing up I thought I had to be perfect. My parents expected me to obey as an example to my siblings, and my church expected me to serve as a leader to the youth. I wanted to please God, so I took on the role of "perfect Carrie," and I was trapped.

Proverbs 29:25 (NLT) says, *"Fearing people is a dangerous trap, but trusting the Lord means safety."* Fear trapped me in anxiety and comparison—which Scripture says is not wise (2 Corinthians 10:12)—and caused me to live in frustration and condemnation. I felt like a failure every time I messed up. In Russia, I still hadn't discovered this secret. I wanted people to like me and be happy I was there. I didn't want to offend or disappoint anyone. But it seemed everyone had a different opinion of how I should be living my life and conducting my ministry.

Listening to those voices and putting too high a priority on people's acceptance negated the love of God in my life. It kept me from fully obeying Him. I became fearful and found myself choosing acceptance over obedience every time. It wasn't until I accepted this revelation of God's love and stopped submitting to other's opinions that I started finding traction in Russia. God's love offered me freedom. It was no longer a big deal if no one else loved me or if someone criticized me. God loved me. And His love gave me the confidence to obey—even when it was uncomfortable.

Love makes it easier to forgive and control our emotions; easier to reject offense. Understanding God's love causes our faith to function on a different level. It gives us the ability to operate in the supernatural where signs and wonders are commonplace. We see the dead raised and the blind receive their sight. We see people step out of wheelchairs, not because we are super saints, but because our focus shifts from ourselves to God.

The Bible says, *"faith working through love"* (Galatians 5:6). In other words, our faith is most active when we focus on God's love. In those moments of clarity, we stop empowering criticism. We stop worrying about the last time we fasted or woke early to read the Word. We stop trying to prove our spirituality and we focus on God. We pray agreeing with God's Word, agreeing with His love—and then watch faith manifest.

Scripture says God delights in showing Himself strong on our behalf (2 Chronicles 16:9). He delights in manifesting His love. When we pray we don't need to worry about saying the right words or quoting the right Scriptures. We just need to know that sickness, poverty, and depression are not of God. Love dealt with those issues on the cross. They are not His will.

> *Beloved, I wish above all things that thou mayest prosper and be in health, even as thy soul prospereth* (3 John 1:2 KJV).

God desires that we experience health, provision, and peace every day of our lives. I remember a time in Russia when money was short and bills were piling up. I needed to buy groceries. Rent was coming due. Salaries needed to be paid. Everything was coming to a head and I didn't know how to deal with it. Riding the bus home one day, I prayed, "Lord, what do I do? You told me to come here, but I'm struggling. It doesn't look like I'm going to make it. I need help." The Holy Spirit began ministering to me saying, "Carrie, I called you here. You didn't come on your own. You came in obedience to Me. That means the groceries, the rent, the salaries, it's all My bill." Sweet relief! God was going to take care of me. Of course, I had to keep reminding myself of that on the ride home.

When anxious thoughts arose such as, *I live in the Arctic Circle… what if they kick me out? I'll freeze,* I had to reassure my heart and "cast my care" upon the Lord knowing He cared for me (1 Peter 5:7). Just like an employer pays employees for their time and covers the cost of materials, God covers the cost of my obedience. God loves me. I was obeying Him. It was His bill.

Thankfully, by the time my dad called that night, I was in a good place. I didn't tell him I needed money. I just kept reminding myself that God was my benevolent Father. He would take care of me. At the end of our telephone conversation, my dad said, "By the way, Mom forgot to tell you that a check came in last week. She deposited $1,500 in your bank account." Hallelujah! That was more than enough to pay rent and buy groceries. God had proven His love for me yet again—He had supplied my need before I even asked Him!

> *Therefore I say to you, do not worry about your life, what you will eat or what you will drink; nor about your body, what you will put on. Is not life more than food and the body more than clothing? Look at the birds of the air, for they neither sow nor reap nor gather into barns; yet your heavenly Father feeds them. Are you not of more value than they? Which of you by worrying can add one cubit to his stature? So why do you worry about clothing? Consider the lilies of the field, how they grow: they neither toil nor spin; and yet I say to you that even Solomon in all his glory was not arrayed like one of these. Now if God so clothes the grass of the field, which today is, and tomorrow is thrown into the oven, will He not much more clothe you...?* (Matthew 6:25-30)

The demonstration of God's care is not just available to missionaries and full-time ministers. God does not show favoritism (Romans 2:11). He does not love in levels. God doesn't love Mike and me any more than He loves you. And He doesn't love you any more than He loves your neighbor. The differences in our experiences lie only in the way we respond to God's love.

Throughout the book of John, the author calls himself *"the disciple whom Jesus loved"* (John 13:23-25; 19:26; 20:2; 21:7,20). But Jesus didn't love John more than the rest of His disciples. He didn't die for John alone. Jesus didn't wash the feet of only those disciples who would stand with Him to the end. He washed everyone's feet. Jesus didn't love John more! But John understood Jesus' love more, and we see that in the way he responded to Jesus. John laid his head on Christ's chest with confidence. He recognized Jesus from far away. And when the other disciples deserted Jesus in the Garden, John stood at the foot of the cross without fear (John 19:26).

The revelation of being loved by God changed the way John responded under pressure, and it should change our response to and interaction with God as well. We don't have to wait for God to declare us the "favorite." We can lay our head on His chest. We can step out in faith staring persecution, grief, and pain in the face (1 John 4:18-19).

We respond to God's love for us by trusting His love for our children and marriages, seeing His love make movement toward our health and finances. When fear rears its ugly head, we recognize it as a warning that our focus has shifted from God's love onto our circumstances, and we repent.

Life FOUNDATION

SPIRIT, SOUL, AND BODY

Now we have received, not the spirit of the world, but the Spirit who is from God, that we might know the things that have been freely given to us by God (1 Corinthians 2:12).

5

Understanding Our Spiritual Makeup

The understanding of God's love is the cornerstone of our spiritual foundation. It provides the lens we need when reading God's Word and keeps our faith from derailing. It gives us the ability to see through difficult circumstances—which are just changeable facts—and respond to them according to the truth of God's Word—which never changes. Out of this foundation of love grows the understanding of our spiritual identity and the true nature of God.

In the third and fourth chapters of Matthew's Gospel, we read how Jesus started His earthly ministry. In chapter three, John the Baptist recognizes Jesus and reluctantly baptizes Him before the people.

> *As soon as Jesus was baptized...the heavens were opened, and He saw the Spirit of God descending like a dove and resting on Him. And a voice from heaven said, "This is My beloved Son, in whom I am well pleased!"* (Matthew 3:16-17 Berean Study Bible)

Notice how the Voice described Jesus as the *"beloved Son."* That was Jesus' identity. It's what gave Him the ability to connect with God and minister to people. In Matthew 4:3, the story continues with Jesus being led by the Spirit into the wilderness. There He fasted and prayed, and after forty days, the *"tempter came to Him."* Now if Jesus were anything like us—and we know He was (Hebrews 4:15)—His mind and body would have been screaming, "Food or die!" in that moment. And in that moment of weakness and preoccupation, the tempter came. For the next several verses, Satan tempts Jesus exactly as he tempts us—in our identity. If Satan can get us to question our identity as beloved children of God, more often than not he will be successful in leading us into sin.

When the tempter came to Jesus saying, *"If You are the Son of God..."* (Matthew 4:3-6), Jesus overcame by citing what was *"written"* in God's Word. He knew His identity. He knew He was more than Mary and Joseph's son. He knew growing up in Nazareth did not limit how God could use Him. He did not allow lust, greed, or pride to distract Him. Instead, Jesus overcame every temptation by responding with the Word—and we can too:

> *But if the Spirit of Him who raised Jesus from the dead dwells in you, He who raised Christ from the dead will also give life* [power] *to your mortal bodies through His Spirit who dwells in you* (Romans 8:11).

The devil does not understand the power of the love of God. He has seen it demonstrated, but he has never partaken of it. When he tempted Jesus in the wilderness saying, *"If you are the Son of God...,"* he left out a key word. When Jesus was baptized, the Voice didn't just call Him a son, the Voice called Jesus the *"beloved Son."* Satan has no idea what that means. He doesn't know what it is to be loved by God. He doesn't understand the power walking in the love of God brings.

While Carrie and I were in Russia, we met an older American lady who woke up one morning with her face sagging. She couldn't close her eyes or her mouth. She literally held everything together with Band-Aids. At the hospital, the doctors told her, "You've been out in the cold. Your face froze. Just warm it up and everything will be fine." Our friend knew she'd had a stroke, so she went to a European clinic. There, they put her on a machine that confirmed her suspicion and discovered she was still having mini-strokes in the back of her brain stem.

As an American in a foreign country who didn't know the language well and had few relationships, she was fearful. But she was also a believer. One day in prayer, the Lord said to her, "Why are you worried? There's never a moment you are not on My heart and in My mind." That reminder of God's love ministered to her and gave her the strength she needed to believe.

We all face hard circumstances in life. But no circumstance— no matter how hard—is greater than God's love. No circumstance trumps Jesus' sacrifice or can weaken the Holy Spirit's work within us. We have to keep our circumstances in their proper perspective. We are complete in Christ (Colossians 2:10). The same Spirit who raised Jesus from the dead, who lived in and empowered Him, lives in us (Romans 8:11). That means everything we read in the Word, everything Jesus did—healing the sick, cleansing the lepers, raising the dead—we can do, if we understand our identity as beloved children of God (John 14:12).

The first step in understanding our identity is learning to recognize our spiritual makeup. Genesis 1:26 says we were created in the image of God. God is a three-part Being: Father, Son, and Holy Spirit (2 Corinthians 13:14). That means we are three-part beings. Paul reiterates this in First Thessalonians 5:23 when he lists our parts as spirit, soul, and body. Unfortunately, many people, scholars included, miss this verse and only identify two parts of our makeup—soul and body. They consider "spirit" and "soul" to be interchangeable words. But they are distinct.

Psalm 139:13 (NIV) says that God created our *"inmost being."* Because God created our inmost being, then we should go to God and His Word to understand it. Hebrews says:

> For the word of God is living and powerful, and sharper
> than any two-edged sword, piercing even to the **divi-
> sion** of soul and spirit, and of joints and marrow, and
> is a discerner of the thoughts and intents of the heart
> (Hebrews 4:12).

The Word of God is the only way to divide soul and spirit. We cannot feel or see their differences apart from it. Andrew Wommack has an amazing teaching on this, but in a nutshell, every believer who has received the grace of God in the person of Jesus Christ has been recreated in His image. Our spirit is now identical to Jesus and full of life (1 John 4:17; John 6:63).

The soul is the other part of our *"inmost being,"* as cited in Psalm 51:6 and 2 Corinthians 4:16. It includes the mind, will, emotions, and conscience; what many call our "personality." The most obvious part of our makeup is the body. Unfortunately, the majority of people—Christians included—spend their whole lives focused on this earth suit rather than our inmost being, our spirit.

When God made man, He formed the body from the dust of the earth and breathed *"the breath of life"* into him (Genesis 2:7). This breath of life was his inward self, a combination of soul and spirit that allowed him to commune with God, reason, make choices, and feel emotions. The breath of life separated humanity from the rest of the animal kingdom. When God made Adam, He created him as a representation of Himself on earth. And as God's representative, he was to live a certain way—directed by the Spirit. Unfortunately the next part of the story, told in Genesis 2:18,21-22, is that Adam and his helper Eve failed, alienating humans from the life of God (Ephesians 4:18). The Godlike Spirit departed and humans began living lives directed by the flesh.

The scriptural term "flesh" refers to our physical body and people's unrenewed souls. It includes things like lust and greed and pride—sin—but it also refers to the way we receive and process information. Being directed by the flesh is being directed or dominated by our five senses.

Before Adam and Eve sinned, they walked with God *"in the cool of the day"* (Genesis 3:8). Nothing hindered their relationship. But after disobeying God and eating of the tree of the Knowledge of Good and Evil, something changed. For the first time, Adam and Eve felt shame. They hid from the Lord.

When God asked Adam why he was hiding, Adam replied, *"I was afraid because I was naked; and I hid myself"* (Genesis 3:10). Adam and Eve had been naked since the day of creation and not feared God! But sin had cut off the flow of life in their spirit. It blinded their spiritual eyes and caused them to see themselves as only physical beings dominated by what they could see, taste, hear, smell, and feel. Adam and Eve's soul—mind, will, and emotions, which at one time were directed by their spirit—was darkened and became enslaved to their body (Ephesians 4:18).

Fast-forward a few thousand years and we see this problem repeated over and over in Scripture. God wants to commune with humankind. But they are dominated by the flesh. People struggle to hear God's voice, struggle to believe and obey. Still God desires relationship and works with humanity as much as possible. We see His Spirit inspire Noah. We watch Him direct Abraham and speak with Moses. The Spirit empowers Samson. He rests upon the prophets and grants wisdom and favor to Daniel.

But until Jesus came, God could not recreate His love relationship with His created beings. He could not indwell a people dominated by sin and directed by the flesh. Then, *"when the right time came..."* the Holy Spirit overshadowed a virgin named Mary.

> *But when the right time came, God sent his Son, born of a woman, subject to the law. God sent him to buy freedom for us who were slaves to the law, so that he could adopt us as his very own children. And because we are his children, God has sent the Spirit of his Son into our*

hearts, prompting us to call out, "Abba, Father." Now you are no longer a slave but God's own child. And since you are his child, God has made you his heir (Galatians 4:4-7 NLT).

Hallelujah! Jesus redeemed us. He broke the power of sin in our lives and restored us to our rightful place in creation—intimate relationship with the Father. So the phrase, "Have you received Jesus?" is not a Sunday school cliché. When we ask that question, we're talking about receiving the Spirit of Christ Himself into our inmost being. That's why Jesus said it was better that He go away (John 16:7). Jesus could have stayed on Earth and lived forever in a physical body, but He would have been subjected to the laws of nature. When Jesus walked the earth, He could only be in one place at a time. A resurrected body wouldn't change that. If Jesus were physically present with us today, He could only live and fellowship with a few of us at a time. He could not live *in* us—but the Holy Spirit can.

That's why, as believers full of His Spirit, we should be living a certain way. We are God's representatives on earth. As Romans 8:9-10 says, *"But you are not in the flesh but in the Spirit, if indeed the Spirit of God dwells in you...And if Christ is in you, the body is dead because of sin, but the Spirit is life because of righteousness."* As believers, the Spirit of God lives in us and empowers us to live as God intended. But like Adam, we still have a choice. We can choose to live our lives directed by the flesh and face the same consequence of death Adam and Eve faced, or we can choose to live life directed by our spirit and experience salvation—God's *zoe* life.

For those who live according to the flesh set their minds on the things of the flesh, but those who live according to the Spirit, the things of the Spirit. For to be carnally minded is death, but to be spiritually minded is life and peace. Because the carnal mind is enmity against God; for it is not subject to the law of God, nor indeed can be. So then, those who are in the flesh cannot please God. But you are not in the flesh but in the Spirit, if indeed the Spirit of God dwells in you. Now if anyone does not have the Spirit of Christ, he is not His. And if Christ is in you, the body is dead because of sin, but the Spirit is life because of righteousness (Romans 8:5-10).

As Christians, we are always *"in the spirit."* Christ dwells in us; our bodies are dead. We are no longer controlled by the flesh—that old self concerned with carnal, natural things. *"We know that our old sinful selves were crucified with Christ so that sin might lose its power in our lives. We are no longer slaves to sin"* (Romans 6:6 NLT). We are new creations in Christ Jesus (2 Corinthians 5:17). Now we must choose whether we will continue identifying with that old self by walking after the flesh and being bound by the parameters of this world's system—or identify with our new self and walk after the Spirit into freedom and joy.

Romans 8:11 says that the Holy Spirit quickens or gives life to our mortal bodies. Beloved, true life and peace come through the Spirit of God, and that life has the ability—the power—to affect our fleshly bodies. When we turn from the things of the flesh and set our minds on the things of the Spirit (the Word of God, what Christ has done for us, and our new identity in Him) our physical bodies start bringing glory to God by displaying His handiwork. Our spirit starts manifesting healing and peace, experiencing supernatural energy, and demonstrating His wisdom and ability in us. That's what Scripture calls walking in the Spirit (Galatians 5:16).

6

Walking in the Spirit

For the purpose of illustration, let's pretend to separate each part of our makeup into three distinct versions of ourselves. Each version will be a fully functioning piece whose decisions affect the other parts. We'll put *spirit* on the right. *Soul* in the middle. And *body* (or flesh) on the left. One more piece of instruction. You must understand that this illustration only applies to believers. Before receiving Jesus, our spirits—part of our inward self—are dead and we are slaves to sin (Colossians 2:13). We can't help but to walk after the flesh. Only faith in Jesus quickens our spirit, giving it life and breaking the bondage of sin and death over us offering us a choice.

> *And you He made alive, who were dead in trespasses and sins, in which you once walked according to the course of this world, according to the prince of the power of the air, the spirit who now works in the sons of disobedience, among whom also we all once conducted ourselves in the lusts of our flesh, fulfilling the desires of the flesh and of the mind, and were by nature children of wrath, just as the others. But God, who is rich in mercy,*

because of His great love with which He loved us, even when we were dead in trespasses, made us alive together with Christ (by grace you have been saved), and raised us up together, and made us sit together in the heavenly places in Christ Jesus, that in the ages to come He might show the exceeding riches of His grace in His kindness toward us in Christ Jesus (Ephesians 2:1-7).

If you remember, *spirit* is the part of our makeup that communicates with God. It is our life-giving part. *Soul* is the part of our makeup that makes decisions. And *body* reacts to outside stimuli. The quickened *spirit* is always tuned to God's voice and ready to obey. It is full of life, love, and power. The *body,* on the other hand, is always aware of physical circumstances. It is tuned to self and is constantly looking for ways to gratify self's needs and desires. (That's not necessarily a bad thing, but it can lead us to sin. For example, if the body didn't alert us to heat, hunger, or danger we'd die. But we all know people—or may be people—who have allowed those legitimate physical needs to morph into selfishness, gluttony, and fear.) These two parts of our makeup are fixed. They are in opposition to one another and desire different things. *"For the flesh desires what is contrary to the Spirit, and the Spirit what is contrary to the flesh..."* (Galatians 5:17 NIV). But the *soul* fluctuates (Romans 8:6; Ephesians 4:14).

For the purpose of this illustration, whenever we mention the word "choose," imagine the *soul* (the part of us that chooses) turning toward either the *body* or *spirit* and walking in that direction.

As believers, when we choose to submit to and focus on physical circumstances, we walk in the flesh and produce carnal results. Our born-again *spirit* is still infused with God's life. It does not cease to exist, but we only experience the things our *body* can see, taste, hear, smell, and feel. If we're hungry, we grump and growl until we find food. If we have bills coming due, we worry and toil until they're paid. But when we *choose* to focus on who we are in Christ, we walk in the *spirit* and produce spiritual results. Our *body's* needs and desires do not cease to exist, but we experience the kind of abundant life the Spirit offers. In other words, our focus determines our direction. Or as Qui-Gon Jinn said in the first episode of *Star Wars*, "Your focus determines your reality." It's true. We can choose to focus on the things we see with our body, or the truth of Christ alive within us.

It's hard to partake of our spiritual inheritance when we're focused on natural things. But if we keep our focus on God and how big He is, our circumstances will seem small and insignificant in comparison. On the other hand, if our focus turns to life's circumstances, those circumstances and the feelings they produce will feel gigantic. We become stressed and overwhelmed. We start looking at ourselves as grasshoppers, and—as the Israelites discovered while searching out the Promised Land—that focus leads to defeat. The *soul* therefore is the pivot point. That's why Paul talks about the need to renew our minds with God's Word:

> *And do not be conformed to this world, but be transformed by the renewing of your mind, that you may*

prove what is that good and acceptable and perfect will of God (Romans 12:2).

The Word of God gives us a picture of who we are in the *spirit*. Many people try to overcome sin and challenges, and try to build a relationship with God by focusing on the *body*. "I'm not going to do this. I'm going to start doing that." But we can't obtain righteousness in the *flesh*. We can't perform well enough, long enough. We can't fix ourselves. Even "super saints" who seem to reflect an image of righteousness and spirituality find themselves frustrated when everything they do comes from the flesh. They start to live life fearing someone will discover their hypocrisy.

The solution is simple: *"Walk in the Spirit, and you shall not fulfill the lust of the flesh"* (Galatians 5:16). In other words, turn around. Pivot. Turn from the flesh and reorient yourself to the Spirit. Go back to God's Word. Discover what it says about your circumstance. Remember who you are *in the Spirit*. This is not about doing all the right things or "earning salvation." You and I can't do anything to earn what God has graciously given. We can't do anything to earn His love. God gives salvation freely; and when we respond to Him in faith, we get to experience its benefits (Psalm 103:2).

This understanding enables us to stand up quickly when we stumble (Proverbs 24:16). Galatians 5:22-23 says the Spirit of God produces *"love, joy, peace, longsuffering, kindness, goodness, faithfulness, gentleness, self-control."* So if I'm not manifesting the fruit of the Spirit—if I'm offended or angry, emotional, or worried—I know my focus is off and I need to turn around. That is the scriptural definition of repentance.

As a Christian, we should not continue living our lives by doing whatever the flesh craves. That's not who we are. We must choose what to set our minds and hearts upon. If we set our minds on the things of the *Spirit*, we will become slaves of righteousness (Romans 6:18). But if we set our minds on the things of the flesh, we will eventually become a slave to sin. The more we focus on the flesh—even as believers—the harder our hearts will become and the easier it will be to fall into the enemy's traps. That's why the Bible says to "guard your heart" (Proverbs 4:23 NIV). Guarding your heart is really guarding your *soul*. It's being careful where you set your attention.

We are always cautious of what we allow our kids to hear and see, and with whom we allow them to spend time. They are still young. They are still learning about these things, so it's our job as parents to help them guard their hearts. One day while we were all at home, Mike and I had several work commitments to attend to, so our kids were watching television. It was an appropriate show for little kids—but apparently the commercials were not. When we checked in on them, both were sitting on the couch with their little hands covering their eyes. We asked what was wrong and they sang out, "We're guarding our hearts." It was so sweet!

Beloved, every lie, every sickness, every temptation the enemy throws at us is designed to force our minds off who we are in the *Spirit* and onto the desires of our *flesh*. We are powerless in the *flesh*. As long as our focus remains there, we're not a threat. We cannot resist the enemy from that position. In the flesh, all we can do is struggle through and hope we make it. What a torturous way to live!

God has given us tools to overcome every situation and circumstance we face—but we must not take our eyes off who we are in the Spirit. In the Spirit, we have all power. We have all authority. Everything we need is there. Every ounce of healing power we could need for the rest of our lives is in our *spirits*. Every bit of wisdom, every grain of peace, it's all waiting for us in the *Spirit*.

First Corinthians 6:17 says our spirits are one with the Father. We are God-possessed. That's not a scary thing; *possessed* simply means owned or controlled by. As believers our *spirits* are possessed by Life; possessed with light and love. The same Spirit who lived in Jesus lives in us. And we have a handwritten invitation, signed in Jesus' blood, to submit to and become one with that Life just as He and His Father are One (John 17:22).

So why do we struggle? If the Spirit of God lives in us, why do we waffle in faith? Because our *souls* are stuck on the habits, thoughts, and attitudes of the *flesh*. The flesh really is capable of anything. What some people have done in the name of Christ is horrifying. But the only way that is possible in the life of a believer, is if we ignore this revelation of our spiritual makeup. We are the temple of the Holy Spirit (1 Corinthians 6:19). He is not far off. He has made His dwelling place in us. He will never leave us nor forsake us (Deuteronomy 31:8). We have the ability to resist temptation. We don't have to be slaves to our *flesh*. We don't have to be sick or depressed. We don't have to be held back by past mistakes. We just have to change the way we think.

That's why our relationship with God's Word is so important. Second Timothy 2:15 (KJV) says, *"Study to shew thyself approved unto*

God, a workman that needeth not to be ashamed, rightly dividing the word of truth." We don't study the Word so God will accept us. We don't study to be proven worthy of His Spirit. We are already approved of Him. We study to show "thyself" approved. We study to prove to ourselves that what God said is true. We study to discover who we are in the *Spirit*.

The Bible shows us how to let the Spirit of God within us become our driving force. When we get sick, the Word reminds us that healing lives in our hearts. There is no room for sickness and disease. When we're full of worry and fear, the Word reminds us of God's love, and that drives fear far from us. The Word renews our minds by shifting our focus back to the *Spirit*. This sounds simple and it really is, but it takes diligence to walk out. It's easy to set our minds on the things of the *flesh*—we've been doing it all our lives. It's easy to feel frustrated when we're struggling with financial pressure or sick bodies. Though we give it to God in prayer, 20 seconds later we may be thinking, *What am I going to do?* In those moments, we must consciously choose to bring *"every thought into captivity"* and pivot back toward the *Spirit*. It may feel like we're waffling in faith, but we're actually fighting a spiritual battle.

> *For though we walk in the flesh, we do not war according to the flesh. For the weapons of our warfare are not carnal but mighty in God for pulling down strongholds, casting down arguments and every high thing that exalts itself against the knowledge of God, **bringing every thought into captivity to the obedience of Christ*** (2 Corinthians 10:3-5).

Nearly every spiritual battle we fight is won or lost in the *soul*. Getting ahold of our minds is spiritual warfare. And every time we do that it is victory! It doesn't matter if we have to repent 100 times in a day. Every time we take control of our *soul* and turn back to the things of the *Spirit,* we win.

Too often we think of ourselves as baby Christians, weak in faith. We think that because we're new to this teaching or new to the things of the Spirit we can't experience the same *zoe* life as those who are farther along in their journeys. And while we all need to keep growing in these *Life Foundations,* the Spirit in us is not a baby spirit. He does not need to grow and mature. Our *soul* may need to, but not our *spirit.* The fullness of the Godhead lives in us (Colossians 2:9-10).

If we are worried and afraid—God's Spirit is not. If we don't know the next step to take—the Spirit does. If we've never raised someone from the dead or seen someone healed—the Spirit has. And when we begin to see ourselves this way—in the *spirit*—and difficult circumstances arise, our spirit will rise up saying, "I've seen this before. I've done this before. God will come through. This is no big deal, *because as He is, so are we in this world'*" (1 John 4:17).

When we understand this dynamic of spirit, soul, and body, it changes our prayer life. We stop asking God to fill us with joy or give us peace because we realize those attributes already live within us. God has given us everything that pertains to live and godliness (2 Peter 1:3). But we only experience those blessings through *"the knowledge of Him."* The enemy may try to tell us that when we mess up, when we turn to the flesh, God can't receive us. He's disappointed or frustrated with us. But God says, "I love you. I'm with you. You don't have to walk this alone. Just return to My love."

God never shuts the door to His presence. We do that when we turn to the flesh. The good news is, returning to the Spirit is easy. We simply remember who we are in Christ. We recognize that our stupid, fleshly decisions are not who we really are—and even more liberating, we understand that this truth also applies to those believers who mistreat us. We realize that their foolishness is a result of their choice to pivot toward the flesh; and in those times, we can respond in grace.

While we were in Russia, one of our translators fell into sin with another student. We knew the two wanted to date and wanted to get married, so we had agreed to mentor them and help hold them accountable as they headed toward courtship. We had regular check-ins with them, but one night as they sat in our living room, they disclosed that they were pregnant. Mike and I were devastated. We'd trusted them, had invested in their lives, and given them responsibility to lead God's people. Their confession felt like a slap in the face. But as much as we wanted to rail at them, we took a deep breath and remembered this foundation.

"We love you," we said. "But more importantly God loves you. Nothing you do could ever separate you from His love." The pair began to cry. "We know you're disappointed in yourselves, you have stumbled, but you are not disqualified. God sees you in Christ. His plans for you have not changed. Are you going to get back up? Are you going to return to the things of the Spirit?"

We didn't excuse their sin. We removed them from leadership and influence over the students. But we did not remove them from our home. We continued to pour into them and disciple them through the process of repentance and restoration telling them, "When the enemy comes against you with condemnation, you're going to have to make a decision. You're going to have to take courage, turn from this regret of the flesh, and look to the Spirit."

We asked them to continue attending school, to learn and grow. And one day they stood before the entire student body and said, "We're sorry. We misused the grace of God and thought to hide our sin. We were wrong. Please forgive us."

"The devil has tried to heap shame and condemnation on our brother and sister," we said, "but we're not going to add to that. They have repented. Now we're going to show them the love of God." The couple eventually married and had a beautiful baby boy. They've since moved to the United States and added three more children to their family. We are so proud of them for choosing to walk in the Spirit!

This was also a wonderful learning experience for our students. They saw repentance in action and were able to extend grace to their brother and sister and watch as God restored them. Some even approached us saying, "We've never experienced anything like this. In Russian churches, you are humiliated in front of the entire body and excommunicated for making a mistake like that. You lose every-thing—your salvation, your calling, everything."

Everyone makes mistakes—sometimes life-altering ones. But in those moments, we have a choice. Are we going to stay there wallowing in guilt and shame? Or are we going to remember our true identity in Christ and return to the things of God's Spirit? In ministry, when we see someone stumble, we also have a choice. Will we minister the good news of reconciliation to them? Or heap condemnation on our brother or sister trying to fix the flesh? When we see believers stumble, let us encourage them to submit to the Spirit. Let us remind them who they are and point them back to the Word. Every one of us has been called to the ministry of reconciliation.

> *Therefore, if anyone is in Christ, he is a new creation; old things have passed away; behold, all things have become new. Now all things are of God, who has reconciled us to Himself through Jesus Christ, **and has given us the ministry of reconciliation**, that is, that God was in Christ reconciling the world to Himself, not imputing their trespasses to them, and **has committed to us the word of reconciliation. Now then, we are ambassadors for Christ, as though God were pleading through us: we implore you on Christ's behalf, be reconciled to God** (2 Corinthians 5:17-20).*

The world is full of hurting people. Our job—whether we serve in the ministry or in the workplace—is to point people to Jesus. We are His ambassadors. So let us implore people to be reconciled to God, understanding what He did for us in Christ. Let us choose to walk in the Spirit.

Life FOUNDATION

HOW GOD SEES US

Behold what manner of love the Father has bestowed on us, that we should be called children of God! Therefore the world does not know us, because it did not know Him **(1 John 3:1)**.

7

The Eyes of Grace

Human beings have a tendency to compare themselves with others. We set a standard of behavior that no one can meet, and are often harsh and unforgiving when we fail. We know we could have done more, worked harder, or not said those things. But as we grow in this understanding of God's love and learn to identify the parts of our spiritual makeup, we also begin to realize that God sees us different from how we see ourselves.

When God looks at us, He doesn't see our faults. He doesn't see our issues. He sees us as righteous, healed, prosperous, and full of joy—all the things we are in the Spirit. James tells us:

> *But be doers of the word, and not hearers only, deceiving yourselves. For if anyone is a hearer of the word and not a doer, he is like a man observing his natural face in a mirror; for he observes himself, goes away, and immediately forgets what kind of man he was. But he who looks into the perfect law of liberty and continues in it, and is not a forgetful hearer but a doer of the work, this one will be blessed in what he does* (James 1:22-25).

Here, James compares God's Word to a mirror that shows us who we are in the Spirit. God's Word shows us how God sees us, what He says about us, and all the good He has planned for our lives. It is the *"perfect law of liberty."* It doesn't show us what we can be if we work hard. It doesn't show us what we'll look like after we've walked with God for ten years. It sets us free by showing us who we are *right now* as believers in Christ.

Unfortunately, we often use the Word of God like a natural mirror, approaching it with the intention of finding our faults. We see ourselves, and others, after the flesh and miss what God sees. We make note the failures and disappointments of our past and use them to disqualify ourselves from God's blessings.

God does not see us through the lens of our past. When God looks at us, He sees through the lens of His past—the cross. We must stop using His Word to uncover our faults. If we belong to Christ, we are fixed. The Holy Spirit lives in us. That means we have access to the same power, the same anointing, and the same intimacy with God that Jesus had. That's what grace is all about.

God loves us. He gave His Son to redeem us so He could make His dwelling place within us. When God looks at us, He doesn't see our flesh and all its imperfections. He sees Himself. He sees grace. Not a grace that frees us to walk in sin without consequence, but Grace—the person of Jesus—who says, "This is not who you are. Get up. Try again. This time, allow My Spirit to lead you, teach you, and guide you into all truth" (see John 16:13). Grace empowers us to change. It reminds us who we truly are and enables us to live life from the Spirit.

Whether we are youth pastors or business owners, teachers or politicians, social workers, mothers, fathers, or musicians, God's plan for each of us is to look like Jesus—to be *"conformed to the image of His Son"* (Romans 8:29). But we limit ourselves. We become so focused on what we're going to *do*, we lose sight of who we are to *be*. God wants us to take off those self-set limits. He wants us to learn to judge our successes and our failures after the *Spirit* asking: Does this success make me who I am? Does that failure change the way God sees me? Does it limit my potential? The answer to each question? No.

We cannot exhaust grace—His mercies are new every morning (Lamentations 3:23)—but that doesn't mean we can do whatever we want. We can't continue to be ugly, lustful, revengeful, and immoral even though God only sees us through the eyes of Grace. Those works of the flesh are not who we are. We are God's children. We are holy and righteous. We are self-controlled and alert. And we need to start agreeing with God by acting like who we are (1 Peter 1:16; 5:8).

We find who we are in the Word. The first three chapters of Ephesians declare what God has done for us in the person of Christ. They recall His love and good plan for our lives—which is grace. But the last three chapters of Ephesians display another side of grace. They remind us that who we are in the Spirit should affect what we do in the flesh.

As children, grace instructs us to honor authority. As wives, grace directs us to encourage our husbands to step into their God-given role of leadership instead of criticizing them. As husbands, grace reminds us that our role does not mean ruling over our wives and children with an iron fist, but loving them and drawing out their gifts and calling. Grace influences the way we treat others and changes the way we resist the enemy.

Grace is not one one-dimensional; it is not greasy. Grace has teeth. It offers everything God is and shows us the right way to live. Grace teaches us to deny ungodliness and lust so that we can *"live soberly, righteously, and godly in the present age"* (Titus 2:12). Grace enables us to live above our circumstances. It removes every excuse of the flesh. No more "too old," "too young," or "too damaged." Grace discards those monikers of the flesh and calls us *"qualified"* (Colossians 1:12), *"complete"* (Colossians 2:10), and *"equipped"* (2 Timothy 3:17). It says we *"can do all things through Christ who strengthens"* us (Philippians 4:13).

> *For no matter how many promises God has made, they are "Yes" in Christ. And so through him the "Amen" is spoken by us to the glory of God* (2 Corinthians 1:20 NIV).

We must learn to recognize and agree with (say "amen" to) the grace of God. God's grace is a gift given to whole world when Jesus said yes at the cross. And in that grace, we find all God's promises wrapped and waiting for us to experience. But in order to see those promises come to pass in our lives and bring glory to God, we have to learn to say amen and agree with God.

Repentance is an important part of the grace-filled life. But repentance is not just sorrow. It's a decision to turn around. When we realize we've been walking in the flesh or not behaving as God's children, repentance turns us back toward the Spirit. When we recognize that we've not been agreeing with God or seeing ourselves as He sees us, repentance changes our mind. It says, "That was stupid. I'm sorry, Lord. I know that's not who I am. You see me as righteous and I'm choosing to agree with that. Help me walk in such a way as to bring You glory."

Repentance is not laborious. We have no need to spend hours on our knees begging for mercy. God doesn't put us on probation. Nor do we have to work our way back to Him. We simply turn around.

Consider the prodigal son (see Luke 15:11-32). He took his inheritance, left his father's house, and spent it all on wild living. When famine struck and his money ran out, Scripture says he came to his senses. The boy repented and returned to his father's house offering to take the place of a servant. But the father looked past his son's mistakes. He covered them with a richly ornamented robe and welcomed him back into his house. Anyone walking past in that moment might have seen some crazy hair, but they wouldn't have seen the pigpen. His robe covered it. That's what God sees when He looks at you, and that is what the enemy sees too. That's why he's constantly trying to get you to turn toward the flesh, open up that robe, and look at the filth of the past. Stay covered. Remember who you are and allow God to wrap you in His robe of grace.

In John 16:8-11, Jesus says the Holy Spirit would convict the world of three things: *"Of **sin, and of righteousness, and of judgment**: of sin, because they do not believe in Me; of righteousness, because I go to My Father and you see Me no more; of judgment, because the ruler of this world is judged."* The Holy Spirit's job is to convict the world of sin—specifically, the sin of not believing in Jesus.

However, that is not His role in a believer's life. Instead of convicting believers of sin, the Holy Spirit convicts us of righteousness. Before Jesus came, the Old Testament priests offered daily sacrifices that covered people's sin. Once a year, the High Priest also entered the Holy of Holies to offer a sacrifice for the entire nation. Those men never rested. They always had more sacrifices to make.

Jesus' sacrifice was different. He offered it *once for all* (Hebrews 9:12), then returned to His Father where we see Him no more. He does not have to go in and out of the Holy Place offering sacrifices again and again like the Old Testament priests.

Jesus made us righteous. And as God's children covered in the evidence of His love—grace—God does not keep track of our wrongs. When we mess up, the Holy Spirit reminds us of our covering. He reminds us of what Jesus did and convicts us of our righteousness. He says, "You're better than this. Don't you know what's in you? Don't you know who you are? I have a plan for you, and this is not part of it. Repent. Return to who you are in the Spirit."

The Holy Spirit also convicts us that the ruler of this world is judged. In other words, Satan is a non-issue. When we focus on who we are in Christ, he has zero authority in our lives. He's been defeated. But sometimes we have to remind ourselves of that. We can't compare what we see in a natural mirror with what we see in God's Word. We have to remind ourselves how God sees us. Sometimes we have to preach to ourselves and declare the Word over our circumstances, over our emotions. We have to tell ourselves to "Get up. Stop whining and feeling sorry for yourself. Turn around. Look to the Father; remember His love and go back to the Word."

When God looks at us, He sees us as righteous, sanctified, and set apart for His good purpose, redeemed. Not recognizing our value in His sight diminishes our effectiveness in the world. First Corinthians 1:30-31 says, *"But of Him you are in Christ Jesus, who became for us wisdom from God—and righteousness and sanctification and redemption— that, as it is written, 'He who glories, let him glory in the Lord.'"* We need to continue to grow in these *Life Foundations—* God's love for us, who we are in the spirit, and how God sees us—so we can truly understand the gospel message and our role in it.

John glimpsed this role while exiled on the Isle of Patmos. When he attempted to kneel before a visiting angel, the angel rebuked him saying, *"See that you do not do that! I am your fellow servant.... For the testimony of Jesus is the spirit of prophecy"* (Revelation 19:10). Notice how the angel tied Jesus' testimony (the past), with prophecy (the future). Jesus' testimony, His entire life's work—every healing, every miracle, every prayer—has become our spirit of prophecy. That means everything we see in the Word that Jesus accomplished is now prophesied or declared over our lives.

Because Jesus fulfilled the law, we can be right with God. Because He bore our sickness and grief, we can be healed. Because we have the same Spirit living in us, we can do what He did. *"As He is, so are we in this world"* (1 John 4:17). What an amazing statement! But have you ever looked at that Scripture in its full context?

> *And we have known and believed the love that God has for us. **God is love**, and he who abides in love abides in God, and God in him. Love has been perfected among*

*us in this: that we may have boldness in the day of judgment; because **as He is, so are we in this world**. There is no fear in love; but perfect love casts out fear, because fear involves torment. But he who fears has not been made perfect in love* (1 John 4:16-18).

We are surrounded by the love of God! We can be like Jesus, we can experience God's goodness and peace and share that goodness with the world because we *"have known and believed"* the love of God.

Do you see how these foundations of God's love, our spiritual makeup, and grace, seeing things from God's perspective, tie together? They are essential elements of our Christian walk. With them, we push past fear and failure and start walking in our full potential. We resist the temptation to compare ourselves with others or measure our value by our position; and instead, determine our value by what God was willing to pay for us—His only Son. We choose to agree with God and measure our success in light of our obedience. And in that, find freedom!

Life FOUNDATION

IDENTITY
IN CHRIST

Therefore, having been justified by faith, we have peace with God through our Lord Jesus Christ, through whom also we have access by faith into this grace in which we stand, and rejoice in hope of the glory of God (Romans 5:1-2).

8

A New Identity

In the book of Exodus, God gave Moses instructions for building His earthly dwelling place. He laid out who Moses should hire to do the work, the type of materials they should use, and the designs they should make. He also told Moses what to carve on the beams, what colors to use in the tapestries, what the priest should wear, and even how to build the mechanisms used to transport the Tabernacle. He left nothing to Moses' discretion. Everything was specifically detailed and everything had meaning—even the nails. For example, God told Moses to sink nails half in and half out to signify the redemption that was coming through His Son who would be both God and man. Everything pointed to what He would accomplish in Christ.

It's amazing to think how purposeful God was in this design. Even the entrance to the Tabernacle was significant. To enter the Tabernacle and meet with God, worshipers had to go through a series of rooms—the inner court, the Holy Place, and finally the Holy of Holies. Three doorways called the "way," "truth," and "life." Years later, Jesus recalled that when He said, *"I am the way, the truth, and the life. No one comes to the Father except through Me"* (John 14:6).

Jesus identified the process by which the priests met God face-to-face saying He was the access point, the Living Tabernacle. That's why the Pharisees became so irate. They weren't willing to make Jesus—whom they saw as just a man—the doorway to God.

But for us who have entered *"the Holiest by the blood of Jesus, by a new and living way which He consecrated for us, through the veil, that is, His flesh,"* we are now His temple (Hebrews 10:19-20; 1 Corinthians 6:19). We may *"draw near with a true heart in full assurance of faith, having our hearts sprinkled from an evil conscience and our bodies washed with pure water"* (Hebrews 10:22). What God did through the cross of Christ was a big deal! It was intricately planned and purposeful. He didn't just give us a "pass." He paid the highest price to make us His dwelling place.

With that in mind, we cannot allow the world to redefine who we are or pressure us into climbing the corporate ladder to find success. Our value and worth is not based on our outward appearance (1 Samuel 16:7). Casey the plumber is not inferior to Taylor the CEO. Jesus died for them both. When Jesus walked the earth, He refused to adopt the world's view of Himself. Instead, Jesus discovered who He was in the Scriptures, which is the same place we turn to discover our identity. God's Word declares who we truly are—not who we can be, not even who we should be—*who we are.* And according to the Word, we are God's offspring (Acts 17:28). We need to allow what we read in the Bible to start transforming the way we see ourselves.

So what if we are struggling with sickness or sin? We turn to the Word. We recognize that staying sick or continuing to sin is not part God's plan for His beloved children, and we stop letting that sickness or sin label us or define who we are. Society loves putting people in boxes. They say if we experience severe mood swings, we're bipolar. If we struggle with alcohol, we're alcoholics. If we get fired, we're a failure. But those things are not the sum total of who we are as God's image bearers.

I remember Andrew Wommack teaching about humility when I was in Bible school. He said, "True humility doesn't put self above or below the Word of God, but believes what the Word says about you and submits to its truth." That struck me. We've all met arrogant people who placed themselves above God's Word.

But I have also met people who constantly placed themselves below God's Word. They relegated all God declared them to be to the category of someday. "Someday I'll be sinless." "Someday I'll be healed." "Someday I'll be bold enough or know enough to share my faith." And I realized that, too, was pride. People who constantly berate themselves and place themselves below God's Word are saying that God's Word is not true. It isn't enough. It doesn't apply to their life.

How often do we that? We may think, *I'm just a mom* or *I'm only a salesclerk,* and we allow that identity to determine the parameters of our lives and dictate our future. If we were truly humble, we would allow God's Word to define who we were—not our experience, our education, or our title. I love these verses in Jeremiah:

> *This is what the Lord says: "Let not the wise boast of their wisdom or the strong boast of their strength or the rich boast of their riches, but let the one who boasts*

boast about this: that they have the understanding to know me, that I am the Lord, who exercises kindness, justice and righteousness on earth, for in these I delight," *declares the Lord* (Jeremiah 9:23-24 NIV).

This Scripture passage doesn't say you can't be strong. It doesn't say you can't be wise or rich. It just says we should not boast or put our glory in those things. We cannot allow our identity to rest in the temporal pleasures or sorrows of this world. A job is what we do, not who we are. A bank account does not dictate our worth. Our identity is found in knowing and understanding God.

I was a homeschooled kid. I didn't attend college. After earning my GED, I went straight to Bible school, then left for the mission field. I had no money, no degree, and no work history outside the family business. Yet God called me to Russia.

In Russia, education is the most important thing. It's how Russians introduce themselves. It's the first thing they ask about at a party and how they judge a person's worth. It doesn't matter if a man works in his chosen field or even has a job—if he has an education, he is worthy of respect. (Believe it or not, I once met a street sweeper with a degree in rocket science!) So when I moved to Russia, I was a bit of an odd duck. Everywhere I went people asked, "какое у вас высшее образование?" Which means, "What is your higher education?"

As a young woman with no college degree or even a high school diploma, all I could respond to that question was, "Jesus." I knew my identity in Christ was bigger than my education, so I chuckled at God's sense of humor and held on to the truth that *"those who seek the Lord shall not lack any good thing"* (Psalm 34:10). I was full of wisdom and equipped for every situation and circumstance (2 Timothy 3:17). I chose to agree with God, and He put me in charge of Andrew's Bible school there—a Bible school filled with international university students, the brightest of their nations. Each one spoke seven or eight different languages and were studying to become doctors, engineers, and lawyers. Some were sons and daughters of kings, UN diplomats, and presidents. It was humbling. But each one received the grace of God and are now serving—in that grace—all around the globe.

As Christians, we are called to be like Jesus—living representations of who God is. Yet how few Christians realize what an honor and privilege that is. To know God, to be so intimate with Him that we understand His heart and follow His ways, that we represent Him properly to the world. It is a privilege to be free of others' opinions; to live above our feelings and not be bound by circumstances. Remember:

> *And we know that **all things work together for good to those who love God, to those who are the called according to His purpose**. For whom He foreknew, He also predestined to be conformed to the image of His Son, that He might be the firstborn among many brethren. Moreover whom He predestined, these He also called; whom He called, these He also justified; and whom He justified, these He also glorified* (Romans 8:28-30).

People who have received the love of God, who are walking in the Spirit, and learning to see themselves as God sees them know that no matter what happens *"all things work together for good."* It is an experiential understanding. But Paul goes on to say:

> **What then shall we say** to these things? If God is for us, who can be against us? He who did not spare His own Son, but delivered Him up for us all, how shall He not with Him also freely give us all things? (Romans 8:31-32)

In order to see all things working together for good, we have to consider what we're going to *"say to these things."* It doesn't matter what the people around us say. It doesn't matter what preachers on TV say. What will *we* say when sickness rises up? What will *we* say when depression knocks at the door? Or when accusations arise? What will *we* say when circumstances shout, "You can't do that!" or the people say, "You don't have the qualifications for that!"? What will our response be then? If we understand that God loves us and is for us, we won't question whether or not things are going to work out.

Paul's question, *"If God is for us, who can be against us?"* is rhetorical. He is summarizing everything we've been learning about God's character and our new identity. We know God is for us. We know we are *"predestined to be conformed"* to His image (Romans 8:29). We know we've been called to relationship with God. We have been justified by Jesus' blood. He took the punishment for our sin. And we have been glorified.

God has placed His Spirit within us and we now have the ability to glorify God in our lives. But we have to decide how we're going to respond. Are we going to say amen to God's promises like Second Corinthians 1:20 admonishes? Or are we going to allow the enemy to steal the birthright of our new identity?

Beloved, it's not enough for God's Word to reveal who we are. It's not enough to hear God's promises declared. If that were enough, we would all be experiencing the *zoe* life of God. We would all look like Jesus. We would all be productive in God's Kingdom. We have to learn to agree with God's Word. We have to receive it, process what it says, and allow it to transform our minds. Every promise of God found its "yes" in Christ. "Yes!" to redemption; "Yes!" to acceptance; "Yes!" to healing, prosperity, and peace. But we have to say amen (2 Corinthians 1:20). Pastors can't say amen for us. Our spouse can't say amen for us. We have to allow Jesus' yes to become part of our identity.

Galatians 2:20 is one of our favorite Scriptures. We use it as a plumb line in our lives, our marriage, and our ministry. It reminds us of who we are and the abilities God has placed within us. It's a picture of grace:

> *I am crucified with Christ: nevertheless I live; yet not I,*
> *but Christ liveth in me: and the life which I now live in*
> *the flesh I live by the faith of the Son of God, who loved*
> *me, and gave himself for me* (Galatians 2:20 KJV).

That is our new identity in Christ, our declaration and boast. Christ lives in us, and every day we're renewing our minds to the truths of God's Word and learning to live out that life by faith. That is the grace of God. God's grace empowers each of us to lay down the mistakes and identities of the past and take up our new identity in Christ. Missionary martyr Jim Elliott said, "He is no fool who gives what he cannot keep to gain that which he cannot lose."[1] No one can hang on to this life forever. No matter what we accomplish or how much money we make, we are all heading toward the grave. Why not give what we can't keep—our lives—back to the Father of life and watch the amazing things He does with it?

Speaking from experience, Carrie and I have traveled the world and met some amazing people. We've seen God take the least of society and make them into the benchmark. It's been incredible to watch. But it's all happened because we said amen. We chose to agree with God. We chose to see ourselves "crucified with Christ." And in that daily surrender, found the grace to live out our calling. Colossians 3:2-3 says, *"Set your mind on things above, not on things on the earth. For you died, and your life is hidden with Christ in God."*

Our relationship with God is no longer about religious rules. Our success is not defined by the world's parameters. That old self—our old identity—is dead. It's useless and unqualified. So why walk after the flesh? Jesus says in John 6:63, *"It is the Spirit who gives life; the flesh profits nothing...."* Our new life—our new identity—is hidden with Christ in God. We are complete in Him (Colossians 2:10). As carriers of His Spirit, we surrender our fears and failures, lay down our own agenda, and trust that God's Word is true. We walk after the Spirit.

Too often, believers miss this dynamic of death when learning about grace and their new identity in Christ. But every time Paul talked about these themes of grace and the finished work of Christ, he also talked about death. He called each of us to recognize that grace requires death to self. It requires humility and submission. Too many Christians want all the promises of God with none of the responsibility. They want the benefits of salvation without the intimacy it calls us to.

But before we can glory in resurrection and all the power and authority that brings, Paul says we have to glory in the cross. We have to be willing to lay down our lives and share in Christ's suffering (Romans 8:17). And though no one likes to talk about this aspect of our faith, the grace of God has called us to self-crucifixion and repentance. It has given us the ability to say no to the flesh (Titus 2:12). Galatians 4:9 says, *"But now after you have known God, or rather are known by God, how is it that you turn again to the weak and beggarly elements, to which you desire again to be in bondage?"*

Beloved, we've been redeemed! Christ freed us from the bonds of sin. Yet every time we turn to the flesh, we return to its limitations. Why would we turn back to that bondage? Why would we turn back to the past or our own agenda? We are not our own. We've been bought with a price.

We should honor God with our bodies (1 Corinthians 6:20). We should put away the misdeeds of the flesh and live in comparison to His Word (Romans 8:13). When we do this, Paul says in the next chapter of Galatians, we walk in the Spirit (Galatians 5:25). Laying down our old identity by crucifying the flesh allows us to take up a new identity in the Spirit—our true identity in Christ (Philippians 3:10-11).

Note

1. "Jim Elliot: Story and Legacy"; *Christianity.com,* June 5, 2020; https://www.leadershipresources.org/blog/christian-missionary-jim -elliot-quotes/; accessed February 8, 2021.

9

A Continual Revelation

Our hope, as you read through *Life Foundations,* is that you begin to see how each of these foundational principles build on and connect with the others. They are not separate concepts. When we understand how much God loves us, we understand the purpose of grace. When we understand grace, we understand that our spiritual makeup—spirit, soul, and body—enables us to be carriers of His Spirit and walk after the Spirit regardless of our circumstance.

We understand that because we carry His Spirit, God does not see our faults and failures. He sees us in the Spirit. He sees our potential. And as we submit to and agree with His word—seeing ourselves as God sees us without excuse or comparison—we are transformed into that potential. We are *"conformed to the image of His Son"* (Romans 8:29), and begin to look and talk and act like Jesus.

But no believer grasps these revelations in one sitting. We all have to grow in them. I know more now, after twenty years of ministry, than I knew when I first graduated Charis Bible College. I have more experience—and a lot more failures—in God's grace. I understand how incredibly patient God is with me. How faithful He is to His

Word. I understand that the Word of God does not change, but my acceptance of and surrender to His Word has. Now when I mess up or don't know how to apply the Word, I don't allow that to derail me. I choose to move forward by faith. I recognize that God's yes in Christ is only activated when I respond with amen.

We could never exhaust the richness of these truths. Though we search their depths the whole of our lives, we never *"attain"*; but we can *"press on toward the goal"* (Philippians 3:12-14). We pray this book sparks a hunger within you to press on, to know Him more. We pray it stirs a desire within you for greater intimacy with the Father. Whether you believe it or not, we all have access to the same walk with God, the same level of intimacy Jesus had. We have all been given the same opportunity to know and experience God—but it starts with our decision to seek Him. Jeremiah 29:10-14 says:

> *For thus says the Lord: After seventy years are com-*
> *pleted at Babylon, I will visit you and perform My good*
> *word toward you, and cause you to return to this place.*
> *For I know the thoughts that I think toward you, says*
> *the Lord, thoughts of peace and not of evil, to give you a*
> *future and a hope. Then you will call upon Me and go*
> *and pray to Me, and I will listen to you. And you will*
> *seek Me and find Me, when you search for Me with all*
> *your heart. I will be found by you, says the Lord....*

Many people quote Jeremiah 29:11, but few read the context of that verse and realize the revelation of destiny is birthed in relationship with God. When we recognize and respond to God's goodness by seeking Him, Scripture says we find Him. He makes Himself known to us by performing His *"good word."*

God is not like earthly authority figures. He is *"gracious and compassionate, slow to anger and abounding in love"* (Nehemiah 9:17 NIV). He is not harsh or strict. He is not a dictator. God is a good Father (Matthew 7:11). He is not distant. He is close to the brokenhearted (Psalm 34:18). And, as His beloved children, we are always on His mind and His thoughts toward us outnumber the sand of the sea (Psalm 139:18). Think about that. There are over 10,000 grains of sand in one handful! How many handfuls of sand do you think there are on one beach? In one desert? On our whole planet? And Scripture says every one of God's thoughts toward us is good. That's amazing!

Psalm 139:16 also says, *"...all the days ordained for me were written in your book before one of them came to be."* Before one day of our life is lived, God knows it. He sees the end from the beginning (Isaiah 46:10). He has it figured out. That's comforting. We don't have to have all our ducks in a row, so to speak. We don't have to know how everything is going to work out. We just need to admit that we're not smart enough to manage on our own and choose to trust the One who is. God knows the thoughts He thinks toward us, and He wants us to know them too. He wants us to know our *"expected end"* (Jeremiah 29:11 KJV).

The New International Version of Jeremiah 29:11 says, *"'For I know the plans I have for you,' declares the Lord, 'plans to prosper you and not to harm you, plans to give you hope and a future.'"* God plans for our future. He plans for our prosperity, and that's not just talking about the finances in our pocket. Prosperity is an all-encom-passing word that includes our health and relationships, our mental well-being, and our impact. God wants our marriages to thrive. He wants our kids to know peace and joy, to be secure in their identity. He wants our relationships to be life-giving and purposeful.

God plans for us to prosper in our vision, to prosper in our faith. Will we choose to seek Him? Will we agree with and submit to His Word? Will we choose to become His representatives? His vessels of peace and joy? Will we be the answer this world is looking for? We can be. In relationship with the One who knows all our tomorrows, we can be that vessel.

Just before Mike and I moved to Russia, communism fell and opened the country to a flood of Western philosophy—including Christianity. Thousands upon thousands of people showed up for Christian crusades and conferences. But those same people showed up for psychic rallies and Jehovah's Witness conventions too. The nation was hungry for spiritual things, yet completely illiterate in God's Word. Because of this, a teaching surfaced that declared God used communism to punish the Russian people for straying from Him. It portrayed God as a harsh dictator, and taught that only proper behavior and good works were pleasing to Him. One lady told me, "For 70 years of my life, I was told there was no God. Now there is a God, but if He's like our leaders, I don't want to know Him." Coming into this environment, Mike and I knew our calling was to teach the people God's true nature and unwavering love.

First John 4:7-8 says, *"Beloved, let us love one another, for love is of God; and everyone who loves is born of God and knows God. He who does not love does not know God, for God is love."* Notice to whom this verse is addressed—*"Beloved."* We are loved of the Most High God who loves us with an intimate, unconditional, always-present, never-ending love. And because of that love, we can *"love one another, for love is of God; and everyone who loves is born of God and knows God."* In other words, we demonstrate God's character to others when we love.

This verse tells us that God doesn't just choose to love. He *is* love. There is a distinct difference. Someone who chooses to love can also choose *not* to love. But to *be* love, there is no other option. Love cannot unlove, neither can God act unlovingly. Does love say one thing and do another? Does love approve of someone then assault them? Does it pull someone close then push them away? Does love ostracize others or make a person sick? No! Love protects. It includes. It is constant. And love is who God is.

People who teach that "God puts sickness on you" have not found that in the Bible. They teach it because it's what they've experienced. Once upon a time they got sick, and in desperation they began seeking God. In turn, they became closer to Him. But they took their response to the sickness out of context and attributed the entire experience to God. That's dangerous. We can't base our belief system on personal experience. It will fail. It will fall far short of the truth. We have to base our belief system on something bigger than ourselves. We have to base it on God's Word.

The Word tells us that God draws us near through His love and goodness, not through punishment (Romans 2:4). The sovereignty of God's doctrine—on which many base their idea that God controls everything—is misunderstood. God is sovereign. He is above all things. He is great and mighty—an all-powerful God—but He does not control every breeze or wave, every thought or action of humankind. Second Peter 3:9 says, *"The Lord is not slack concerning His promise, as some count slackness, but is longsuffering toward us, not willing that any should perish but that all should come to repentance."* Yet how many people die and go to hell every day? They aren't dying in sin because Jesus didn't do all that was necessary to save them.

God gave humankind the will to choose right and wrong. He gave us jurisdiction over the earth (Genesis 1:26-28; Psalm 115:16). Humans are in charge of what happens here on earth, but that does not mean God is distant or unaware of our suffering. Throughout history, God has intervened on behalf of His people—to the point of sending His own Son—and He continues to work for our good. God is sovereign above all, but He does not "allow" evil. Neither is He mysterious and unapproachable.

There was a little old lady in charge of monitoring the comings and goings of our apartment building in Russia. And she was always frowning. Every time we passed her desk, she had a sour look on her face. One day as I was signing in I said, "Isn't it amazing that we can know God?" She scrunched up her face up and said, "Young lady, no one can know God. Such pride that you would presume to know God!" She got so mad, but I wasn't offended. Instead, I walked away from that encounter praising God for the privilege of knowing Him and determined to show that little lady God's true character.

Beloved, we can know God. We can know His heart and will toward us. We can know the plans He has for us. We can experience

His goodness. We may never know *all* there is to know of God, that is why we purpose to keep growing, to keep discovering. When people say, "You never can tell with God," they don't know Him. They don't have a revelation of how good He is. They don't have a relationship with Him through reading His Word. Remember what Jeremiah said?

> *But those who wish to boast should boast in this alone: that they truly know me and understand that I am the Lord who demonstrates unfailing love and who brings justice and righteousness to the earth, and that I delight in these things. I, the Lord, have spoken!* (Jeremiah 9:24 NLT)

God is not distant. He is not schizophrenic. He doesn't pretend to love us one day and hurt us the next. He does not give us the grace for salvation then withhold His grace for healing or peace. God wants us to know Him, to trust Him. So He reveals Himself to us through His Word. Psalm 138:2 says God has exalted His Word above His name. That means what He says in His Word, He will do. You can trust God to keep His word spoken through the Holy Spirit into those who wrote the Scriptures. The writer of Hebrews says it is impossible for God to lie (Hebrews 6:18). He does not speak one way and act another. He does not make a promise and leave it unfulfilled.

> *God is not human, that he should lie, not a human being, that he should change his mind. Does he speak and then not act? Does he promise and not fulfill?* (Numbers 23:19 NIV)

*My covenant I will not break, nor alter the word that
has gone out of My lips* (Psalm 89:34).

God's Word can be trusted. And so can His love. Deuteronomy
4:24 calls God's love a *"jealous"* love. That's not the ugly-green-mon-
ster type of jealousy, but the fiercely protective type of jealousy.
God's love would do anything to protect us, anything to provide for
us. Like a husband jealous over his wife, unwilling that anyone would
hurt her or take his place, so God's love is jealous for us. It says, "I
don't want anything in this world to keep you from Me."

But if we don't know this about God's nature, how can we portray
Him honestly to the world? How can we give a reason for the hope
we profess (1 Peter 3:15)? Or stand against false doctrines that say
God is willing to make us sick or kill our children? That He'd do bad
things to draw us closer to Himself? God is so much better than that!
His love is jealous for us. His will is only good. And if we're going to
display His goodness and nature to a lost and hurting world, we have
to know what that nature looks like.

Life FOUNDATION

THE TRUE NATURE OF GOD

This is what the Lord says: "Let not the wise boast of their wisdom or the strong boast of their strength or the rich boast of their riches, but let the one who boasts boast about this: that they have the understanding to know me, that I am the Lord, who exercises kindness, justice and righteousness on earth, for in these I delight," declares the Lord (Jeremiah 9:23-24 NIV).

10

Understanding God's Nature

Many different philosophies of God's nature float around society, even among believers. Some say God is mysterious, a Being that can't really be known. Many think Him authoritative and moody, an unpredictable mix of mercy and judgment. Others say He is all-powerful but distant and uninterested in our day-to-day lives. Still others claim that God loves so desperately, He overlooks evil like a permissive parent. Who is right? How can we know? We have to find out what God says about Himself. We have to go to His Word.

In Middle Eastern culture, names have deeper implications than in Western society. They are more than just a way to get someone's attention. Names are synonymous with a person's character. Similarly, a study of God's names offers insight into His character. The first name of God we're introduced to in Scripture is Elohim (Genesis 1:1). Elohim is an unusual word. In Hebrew, it denotes both singularity and plurality of nature. It points to our God as the triune One—the one Creator-God revealed in three distinct persons.

Then, in Genesis 2:4, God calls Himself YHWH Elohim, which is sometimes translated as Jehovah Elohim. YHWH is the relational name of God (Exodus 3:15). It points toward His interactions with humankind as the "I AM," the ever-present God.

Throughout the Old Testament, we see God revealing Himself to people one facet at a time. He introduced Himself to Abraham as El-Shaddai, the almighty God sufficient to meet the needs of His people (Genesis 17:1-2). Then to Moses as Jehovah-Rapha, the Lord who heals (Exodus 15:26). He also instructed Moses to share this name with the Israelite people: Jehovah-Mekaddish, the Lord who sanctifies (Exodus 31:12-13).

Later, God introduces a "branch" of David through the prophet Jeremiah known as Jehovah-Tzidkenu, the Lord our righteousness. This "righteous branch" would be the One who justifies—the One in whom all things are made "right" (Jeremiah 23:6). And finally, we see God calling Himself Jehovah-Shammah, the ever-present One, the Lord who is "there" (Ezekiel 48:35).

Others knew God by different names. When God offered an alternate sacrifice for Abraham's son on Mount Moriah, Abraham called God Jehovah-Jireh—the Lord who provides (Genesis 22). When the Israelites defeated the Amalekites in their first military victory in Canaan, Moses called God Jehovah-Nissi—the Lord our banner (Exodus 17). Gideon knew God as Jehovah-Shalom—the Lord is peace—after God appeared to him in Ophrah and instructed him to destroy his father's idols (Judges 6). David called God Jehovah-Rohi—the Lord my Shepherd (Psalm 23). Many Old Testament writers saw God as Jehovah Sabaoth—the Lord of hosts (or as we would say "the God of angel armies"). But these names only represent a fraction of God's multifaceted character.

God showed us His whole heart in Jesus. The writer of Hebrews calls Jesus *"the express image"* or exact representation of God (Hebrews 1:3). The Holman Christian Standard Bible says, *"The Son is the radiance of God's glory and the exact expression of His nature...."* Jesus gave us a tangible expression or picture of God's nature. He perfectly displayed God's multifaceted character—not just a portion of it. The Old Testament saints didn't know God fully. They saw His might. They knew His standard of justice and purity. Some even witnessed His mercy. But we can experience more than just God's power and justice. Because of Jesus, we can know the whole of God's character—we can experience His father-heart and know His love and grace.

Unfortunately, many in the Body of Christ have thrown out all that God revealed Himself to be in the Old Testament. They have latched onto His heart of grace and dismissed the rest of His character as if it ceased to exist. But just as God was gracious in the Old Testament, so is He righteous and holy in the New. He has not changed. He is the same yesterday, today, and forever (Hebrews 13:8). Grace does not allow us to live in sin as if the things done in our body don't matter. Grace has not changed God's heart. He is still the God of righteousness, justice, and purity. Grace simply allowed Jesus to meet God's standard of righteousness on our behalf so we could have relationship with God.

Psalm 103:12 says, *"As far as the east is from the west, so far has He removed our transgressions from us."* This verse was inspired by the rules for Old Testament worship. God instructed Moses to set up the Tabernacle from east to west and direct the Israelites to enter from the east side. As they worshiped, the people moved through the Tabernacle singing, praying, and offering sacrifices before exiting on the west side. At that point, their sins were removed *"as far as the east is from the west"* and they left the Tabernacle holy. But their holiness did not last. When the Old Testament saints messed up, they couldn't run back to the Tabernacle pointing to that old sacrifice. They had to run to the closest sheep pen and seek out a new sacrifice (Hebrews 10).

Jesus' sacrifice was different. Knowing we were hopelessly inadequate on our own, God came down to our level to bring us up to His. God *"made Him* [Jesus] *who knew no sin to be sin for us, that we might become the righteousness of God in Him"* (2 Corinthians 5:21). Jesus' sacrifice dealt with the human heart. His sacrifice made us holy *"once for all"* and gave us direct relationship with the Father (Hebrews 10:12-14).

In Jesus, God chose to forget our sin. He cast our sin into the *"depths of the sea"* where He will *"remember no more"* (Micah 7:19; Hebrews 8:12). What happens when you throw a cup of fresh water into the ocean? Can you dip it out again? No. It is swallowed up. It becomes part of the salty sea. The same is true of our sin. It has been thrown into the ocean of God's grace and swallowed up. If you try to dip it out again, all you will find is Jesus' sacrifice—for we have been made righteous.

Beloved, we don't need to fear God—even when we make a mistake. We can run *"boldly to the throne of grace, that we may obtain mercy and find grace to help in time of need"* (Hebrews 4:16). When our children mess up, we teach them to come to us for help. We don't want them to hide in fear, afraid of telling us what happened. We love them. We want to help them walk through their failure with dignity and teach them to do better. God wants the same for us. He wants to help us walk through our mistakes with grace. He wants to teach us what is right and celebrate with us as we grow up in Him (Ephesians 4:15).

One day, a few years ago, we received a phone call just before our daughter came home from school. She'd been sent to the principal's office for punching a boy. When Ellie got home, we brought it up. "You punched a boy, huh?" we said. But Ellie didn't want to talk about it. Embarrassed, she hung her head. "Look, no matter what happened today or what happens in the future, we're going to love you. But we need to talk about this." Ever so slowly, Ellie began to tell us what happened. Apparently, this boy had called her an ugly name like stupid-doo-doo-head or something, so she punched him. We took the time to work through it all; but like God, our focus in that moment was relationship not punishment. Our goal was a change of heart.

That is how correction with God works. When something happens or we make a mistake, we run *to* Jesus, not away from Him. Yes, there is discipline, but God's priority in the discipline is relationship (Proverbs 3:12; Revelation 3:19). Hebrews 12:5-6 (NIV) tells us God disciplines everyone He accepts as His son or daughter:

> *And have you completely forgotten this word of encouragement that addresses you as a father addresses his son? It says, "My son, do not make light of the Lord's*

discipline, and do not lose heart when he rebukes you, because the Lord disciplines the one he loves, and he chastens everyone he accepts as his son."

The King James version of this passage uses the words *chasten* and *scourge*. Those words sound harsh and contradictory to all we've been learning about God's character, but they are not. *Chasten* simply means to correct. Paul uses the same Greek word in Second Timothy 3:16 when he says God's Word is profitable for correction and instruction in righteousness. The word *scourge* means to whip or flog a victim strapped to a pole. Have you, as a child of God, ever been flogged while strapped to a pole? I never have, but Jesus was. He carried the penalty of our sin and was *scourged* on our behalf (Isaiah 53:3-5). Now we receive God's chastening without punishment. We are corrected with His Word. Second Timothy 3:16-17 (NLT) says:

All Scripture is inspired by God and is useful to teach us what is true and to make us realize what is wrong in our lives. It corrects us when we are wrong and teaches us to do what is right. God uses it to prepare and equip his people to do every good work.

God disciplines us—He corrects us—but He does it through His Word. He does not treat us as our sins deserve (Psalm 103:10). He reminds us who we are. He reminds us that we are the righteousness of God in Christ Jesus (2 Corinthians 5:21). He reminds us that we are His beloved children; and as God's children, we are called to reflect His nature and character: *"Then Jesus answered and said to* them, *'Most assuredly, I say to you, the Son can do nothing of Himself, but what He sees the Father do; for whatever He does, the Son also does in like manner'"* (John 5:19). The more we understand God's nature, the easier it becomes to love as He loved, to forgive as He forgave, and to serve as He served; it becomes easier to recognize His voice and leading, and to resist the devil. We become a funnel for the Spirit of God to flow through, and our lives change effortlessly.

When the Lord showed me His character as revealed through His Old Testament names, He did so in the context of my new identity in Christ. He showed me that all those aspects of His character—His Spirit—live in me. Jehovah-Rapha is not just the Lord who heals, but the Lord *my* Healer. And that Healer lives in *me*. Jehovah-Jireh is not just the Lord who provides, but the Lord *my* Provider who has taken up residence in *me*.

When the enemy attacks my body with sickness, he's not just attacking *my* body; he's attacking the very nature of God within me. When the enemy whispers lack to my pocketbook, he's not just trying to steal my finances; he's trying to steal from Jehovah-Jireh living in me. That changes things. The enemy is constantly trying to derail my faith by making me doubt God's character, and God's character in me. If he can get me to question God's goodness and love, he can steal my peace, he can kill my hope and destroy my family. I have to remember:

> *The thief does not come except to steal, and to kill, and to destroy. I have come that they may have life, and that they may have it more abundantly* (John 10:10).

Jesus gave us a succinct definition of God's true nature: God is good; the devil is bad. It's that simple. Anything that brings destruction to our life is not from God. God only gives life. He never makes us sick. The devil is the author of sickness. God never steals our children. The thief does that.

There should be no doubt what equates to *"abundant life."* Lack is not abundant life. Fear is not abundant life. Depression, addiction, confusion...none of those things are part of an abundant life. When we really know God, when something bad happens we will not think, *How have I offended God?* We will recognize the enemy's handiwork. When we really know God, we will not question His leading when we feel His call. If God asks us to do something—like go to Bible college or move to Russia—we wouldn't wrestle over the outcome. We would surrender, trusting in His goodness and provision—and we would know peace.

Years ago, Carrie and I held a youth conference where we spoke about the beauty of surrender. We both gave our testimony: how before we met, God called each of us to surrender our futures (including our marriages) to Him. A young person approached Carrie afterward to say, "I can't do that. I can't trust God with that area of my life." When Carrie asked why he felt that way, the guy said, "Because God could give me somebody ugly." What a low opinion of God! Yet how many Christians think the same way?

Dear friend, when you surrender an area of your life to the Lord, you reap back more than you could ever get on your own! I'm a living testimony of that. I was three years from qualifying for a pension as a correctional officer when Carrie and I met. Had I continued down that path, I would have retired before the age of 50 and would never have had to work another day in my life. But God called me to the mission field. As I was wrestling over the timing of that call, He asked me, "Where's your trust? In the state correctional system, or in Me?"

When I surrendered the whole of my life to God and took that step, I didn't just gain a hope for the future. I experienced His joy and peace in the moment. And it was the best decision I ever made—God gave me a beautiful wife, a wife who has blessed and helped me more than I can describe. He opened doors of ministry for me that I never dreamed possible, simply because I chose to surrender.

Don't be deceived, my dear brothers and sisters. Every good and perfect gift is from above, coming down from the Father of the heavenly lights, who does not change like shifting shadows (James 1:16-17 NIV).

Life FOUNDATION

BELIEVER'S AUTHORITY

Whoever believes and is baptized will be saved, but whoever does not believe will be condemned. And these signs will accompany those who believe: In my name they will drive out demons; they will speak in new tongues; they will pick up snakes with their hands; and when they drink deadly poison, it will not hurt them at all; they will place their hands on sick people, and they will get well (Mark 16:16-18 NIV).

11

God's Image Bearers

The devil hates that we are created in God's image. He hates that we are carriers of God's nature. The devil has been trying to stamp out God's image on earth since the Garden of Eden. He even tried stamping it out in Jesus—but Jesus overcame and gave us the shared privilege of displaying God's image and demonstrating His goodness to the world. Some Christians find that intimidating. But we make things too complicated.

As mentioned previously, Galatians 5:22-23 says the fruit—or byproduct, the natural outflow—of the Spirit is *"love, joy, peace, long-suffering, kindness, goodness, faithfulness, gentleness, and self-control."* That's not a list of traits we have to produce. It is the nature of God in us and toward us. God is love (1 John 4:16). He rejoices over us with gladness (Zephaniah 3:17). His thoughts toward us are peace (Jeremiah 29:11). He is patient and kind to us (2 Peter 3:9; Hosea 11:4). His goodness and faithfulness endure forever (Jeremiah 33:11). He gently draws us to Himself (Jeremiah 31:3). And God is the epitome of self-control as He faithfully executes both justice and mercy in our lives (Matthew 23:23).

Now, because His Spirit lives in us, we can walk out His nature naturally. We can love our enemies and rejoice in persecution (Matthew 5). We can experience peace in the midst of life's storms (Philippians 4:7). We can be patient with our children, kind to strangers, and good to our bosses—not because we strain and strive to do what is right, but because those characteristics are part of our nature. Jesus says in John 15:4-5:

> *Abide in Me, and I in you. As the branch cannot bear fruit of itself, unless it abides in the vine, neither can you, unless you abide in Me. I am the vine, you are the branches. He who abides in Me, and I in him, bears much fruit; for without Me you can do nothing.*

No tree branch has the power in itself to bear fruit. We might be able to get results, but we don't bear fruit. One year, Mike and I flew home from Russia on furlough. We got in late one evening and crashed. The next morning, my parents woke us up to burn tumbleweeds. (Burning tumbleweeds with jet lag is not wise—just in case you were wondering.) We worked all day, crashed again, and were awakened the next morning to cut firewood. Again, we worked all day, slept hard, and were awakened to work a 12-hour shift in my parent's store. And though we tried to do it all with a good attitude, I'm sure we failed. We got results, but we didn't produce fruit.

We can make something happen. We can do things for God; we can bring people together, build ministries, and look successful on the outside, but what we do when the storms come reveals our fruit. Self-effort doesn't last, fruit does (John 15:16).

We have no power to bear fruit or display God's image within ourselves. Only by staying connected to the root—by focusing on our relationship with God and acknowledging who we are in Christ—can we bear fruit. But instead of focusing on relationship with God, too many Christians spend their time worrying about the enemy. They think if they can figure out where the enemy is hiding, they will avoid his traps and open the way for unhindered relationship with God. They spend all their energy determining if this or that person is the enemy; if this movie is demonic; if that promotion is a trick meant to make them lose sight of God. Friend, if that's you, stop wasting time! Stop looking for the devil. Look to Jesus (Hebrews 12:2). Stay connected to the Root. Get to know God and it will be easy to detect what is counterfeit.

The United States government does not train currency officers to spot counterfeit bills by teaching them all the ways counterfeiters create bogus money. Instead, they ensure their officers are experts in recognizing genuine currency. Because these officers know what real bills look and feel like, they can spot counterfeits in seconds.[1] The same is true in our relationship with God. When we know the true nature of God, it is easy to discern the enemy. When doubt whispers in our hearts, we trust God's nature, rebuke the enemy in Jesus' name, and bring every thought into captivity (2 Corinthians 10:5).

Just the other day, our son told us that a teacher at school said, "Sometimes God makes us sick to teach us a lesson." When we asked him what he thought about that, our son didn't waffle or even consider, he simply said, "That's stupid!" Our son has the essence of God's character hidden in his heart. He knows God is good and that

He only does what is good. Life would be so much easier if we all remembered that simple fact. It would be easy to distinguish good from evil. It would be easy to recognize God's handiwork and discern the enemy's.

When we understand God's character, we know His will. We know God would never leave us nor forsake us (Deuteronomy 31:6). We know He is for us, that He promised to lead and guide us (Isaiah 30:21). We know He will provide for our needs (3 John 1:2). And that knowledge changes our prayer life. We don't have to beg for those things or try to prove we are worthy of them. We simply bring our needs before the Father, knowing He hears us and that our prayers are effective (1 John 5:15; James 5:16).

That is profound. Too often, we pursue relationship with God for the gifts He gives instead of for who He is. Once we have what we want of Him, we begin to neglect our relationship and slowly detach from our root system. We forget that the blessings of God flow out of relationship with Him. They are an extension of who He is. Jesus said to, *"seek first the kingdom of God and His righteousness, and all these things shall be added to you"* (Matthew 6:33). In context, those "things" are our physical needs. And according to what Jesus said, *"Your heavenly Father knows that you need all these things"* (Matthew 6:32). In other words, as God's children, they are ours automatically.

We don't have to live a "normal" life like everybody else. We don't have to worry about healing, provision, or any other need that arises in life. We can walk in the supernatural. Though the devil may have painted a target on our back, he cannot separate us from God's love. He cannot separate us from our rightful inheritance. We can display

God's image—His nature and character—every moment of every day. Paul wrote to the church in Rome, as children of God we are *"more than conquerors through Him who loved us"* (Romans 8:37).

> *For I am persuaded that neither death nor life, nor angels nor principalities nor powers, nor things present nor things to come, nor height nor depth, nor any other created thing, shall be able to separate us from the love of God which is in Christ Jesus our Lord* (Romans 8:38-39).

Nothing can separate us from our root system in Christ. Nothing. Not sickness. Not persecution. Not fear or any other enemy attack. When Satan hits us with sickness or fear, we hit right back. We stand our ground. For example, when I'm fighting a cold, I do not detach from my root system. I do not think of myself as the sick trying to get well. I don't pray as if I have to pull healing into my body. I remember who I am. I remember who lives in me and that healing is part of my inheritance. There is no room in my body for sickness. So I think of myself as the healed and I rebuke sickness in Jesus' name. I command it to leave my body.

Do you see the difference? My fight of faith starts from the position of victory. The enemy may be trying to push me out of that position, but I push right back. I protect my inheritance. The same is true when I need to protect my prosperity, my peace, or my joy. Whatever the enemy throws at me, I lift up the shield of faith and remember who gave me my position. I remember who lives in me, who I represent. And I stand fully armed! (See Ephesians 6:13-18.)

God has equipped every one of His children with that same spirit of faith. When faced with hardship, we don't give the enemy a single inch because Jesus made us victorious. That's who we are. Faith is not just a gift God gives us. It's who He is and who He is in us. He *is* peace. He *is* joy. He *is* prosperity. He *is* provision and healing. When we feel ill or we are facing uncertainty, we don't pray, "God heal me if it be Thy will. Give me peace. Show me Your love." No. We know God's will. We know His character and our inheritance as His children. And we must stop letting the enemy steal from us.

> **Fight the good fight** for the true faith. **Hold tightly to the eternal life** to which God has called you, which you have declared so well before many witnesses (1 Timothy 6:12 NLT).

We have to hold tightly to our inheritance of God's *zoe* life. We have to fight from our position of victory. We are God's image bearers, but we cannot become careless with the grace we've been given. We cannot let down our guard simply because we know these truths. We must remain sober and vigilant (1 Peter 5:8). There is an enemy seeking whom he may devour. If we allow the circumstances and monotony of life to distract us—if we lean toward the flesh responding to all the flesh feels and sees—we won't be able to resist him. We won't even recognize him until it is too late. As someone has said, "Give the devil an inch and he'll become your ruler." But every time we fight that good fight—every time we see the fruit of our faith—we become a testimony of God's character to the people around us.

Before going to Charis Bible school, I worked in the federal prison system. For seven years, I bounced between shifts and learned the concept of authority. Though the prison I worked for housed more than 2,000 inmates, we never had more than 128 guards on shift at once. (As a matter of fact, when I worked third shift, there were only 48 non-inmates in the entire building!) Can you imagine the chaos if a fight broke out? Even if every guard employed by that prison happened to be there at the same time, we still would have been vastly outnumbered. But that's not what gave us the authority to control those inmates. Our authority came from the one we represented. It came from justice system of the United States of America.

I saw this same principle at work in Russia. When Carrie and I lived in Russia, police officers stood on the side of the road directing traffic with nothing but a stick. If someone was speeding or made an illegal U-turn, all that police officer had to do was point his stick and the driver would pull over. It was amazing. That police officer didn't have the physical strength or even firepower to make a 2,000-plus-pound car pull over, but the officer did have the authority.

The same is true in our lives. We don't have the physical strength to withstand the enemy's attacks. Neither do we have the power to force our desires into existence. But as beloved children of God, in submission to His Word, we do have the authority. Authority is not a reflection of personal power. It is the right to represent the One who sent you. It's the responsibility to enforce a higher position. As God's image bearers, we have been given the authority to demonstrate His goodness to others, to enforce His will on earth. It doesn't matter what our talents and abilities are; it's not about our personal strength. It's about His.

During His ministry, Jesus delegated authority to the disciples. He told them to cast out demons, heal the sick, raise the dead, cleanse the leper, and preach the Kingdom (Matthew 10:8; Luke 9:1-2). In essence, He told them to display God's character to the world. Jesus repeated that commission, and gave it to us just before He departed.

> *And Jesus came and spoke to them, saying, "All authority has been given to Me in heaven and on earth. Go therefore and make disciples of all the nations, baptizing them in the name of the Father and of the Son and of the Holy Spirit, teaching them to observe all things that I have commanded you; and lo, I am with you always, even to the end of the age." Amen* (Matthew 28:18-20).

Beloved, the life of faith and faith-filled ministry comes out of the overflow of our relationship with God. As we grow in these basic principles of God's Word—these *Life Foundations*—our lives will transform. We will start to see ourselves as God sees us and naturally begin reflecting that identity to the world. We are God's image bearers. We have the authority and power to change the world.

Note

1. Tim Challies, "Counterfeit Detection," June 27, 2006; https://www.challies.com/articles/counterfeit-detection-part-1/; accessed February 8, 2021.

12

Built to Overcome

Each of the concepts within *Life Foundations* feeds into the next. They truly create the structure needed to understand and experience the victory of the Christian life. As we grow in them, our feet become planted on the sure foundation of the Gospel—which is Christ—and we develop an understanding of our spiritual authority.

When we know God and know our identity in Christ, we recognize the enemy when he attacks, and we respond in faith. We become weapons against him. We don't pray amiss. We don't use the name of Jesus like a wish or a magic wand. We understand that when we pray, God hears us because of what Jesus accomplished in His death and resurrection. And we understand that, like Jesus, our prayers will be answered because every word we speak is backed by the authority of Heaven.

Can you imagine what the angels were thinking as they watched God create the world? I imagine an angel looking at the pile of dirt God created with forming man and saying, "Wait! That's You—You're him. What does this mean?" The first chapter of Genesis tells us what it means. God created man in His image to *"have dominion,"* or authority, over the earth and display His nature (Genesis 1:26). Then, after creating mankind, the Bible says God *"blessed them"* saying:

> *Be fruitful and multiply; fill the earth and subdue it;*
> *have dominion over the fish of the sea, over the birds*
> *of the air, and over every living thing that moves on the*
> *earth. ...I have given you every herb that yields seed*
> *which is on the face of the earth, and every tree whose*
> *fruit yields seed...and it was so* (Genesis 1:28-30).

But as Adam began to take his God-given place on the earth, Satan got jealous. He saw God's character and authority in Adam, and he wanted it for himself. In Genesis 3, Satan came to Eve as a wily serpent and said, *"Did God really say you must not eat the fruit from any of the trees in the garden?"* He twisted God's words about the tree of Knowledge of Good and Evil. Then he got Eve to question God's character, and she and Adam ate the fruit from the tree. They fell into Satan's trap and began striving for what had already belonged to them—being like God (see Genesis 3:5-8 NLT).

Adam and Eve missed the mark; they sinned and death entered the world. Disobedience separated them from the life of God, yet God continued to love them. He met with them and made clothes to cover their nakedness and shame, the reason they gave for hiding themselves from His presence (Genesis 3:10). God removed Adam and Eve from the Tree of Life so they wouldn't have to live in a fallen sin state forever (Genesis 3:24), then set in motion a plan of redemption (Genesis 3:15; Revelation 13:8).

So we see this fight for authority from the beginning. God gave Adam authority. Satan wanted that authority and so deceived the man and woman. The humans believed Satan's lies and surrendered authority to him. So God sent Jesus into the world to redeem human-kind and return them to their rightful place of authority.

When Adam sinned, sin entered the world. Adam's sin brought death, so death spread to everyone, for everyone sinned. ...Now Adam is a symbol, a representation of Christ, who was yet to come. But there is a great differ-ence between Adam's sin and God's gracious gift. For the sin of this one man, Adam, brought death to many. But even greater is God's wonderful grace and his gift of for-giveness to many through this other man, Jesus Christ. And the result of God's gracious gift is very different from the result of that one man's sin. ...Yes, Adam's one sin brings condemnation for everyone, but Christ's one act of righteousness brings a right relationship with God and new life for everyone... (Romans 5:12-18 NLT).

Since the enemy stole authority from a man, God had to get it back through a Man. So Jesus came to earth as the perfect Man. He lived and died as our substitute, so when "all authority" was given to Him in resurrection, He—as both fully God and fully man—could legally give it back to us satisfying the Father's heart of mercy and justice (Matthew 28:18). But, like Adam and Eve, if we choose to believe the enemy's lies, we forfeit God's life in that area and sur-render our authority back to the devil. Only now, Jesus doesn't have to die to return that authority to us. He already did that. We simply repent and believe.

That's why the psalmist said, *"Your word I have hidden in my heart, that I might not sin against You"* (Psalm 119:11). The Holy Spirit speaks the language of God's Word. If we're not putting His Word in our hearts, we won't hear when He speaks or be able to recognize the enemy's lies. Knowing God's Word and character protects us. When the doctor says, "You have stage four cancer," we can choose to believe God's Word over our circumstance. We can say, "But God's Word says I was healed at the cross. Healing lives in me, and that is greater than any sickness. I choose to believe God."

Every time the enemy whispers to our hearts, we have that choice. We can believe the lie and surrender our authority, or we can choose to believe God's Word. We can curl up with our blankets and chicken noodle soup and waste the weekend binge-watching Netflix, or we can take the authority Jesus died to give us, resist the devil, and watch him flee.

James 4:7 says, *"Therefore submit to God. Resist the devil and he will flee from you."* But many Christians believe their only weapon against the enemy is time. They think if they can just out-weather the storm, everything will be okay. It might. But relying on that strategy creates wounded Christians. God wants better for us than that. He wants us to know these *Life Foundations* and walk in victory.

When we submit to God—when we choose to believe His Word—and resist the devil, James 4:7 says he *will* flee. It doesn't say he *might* flee. It doesn't say he'll flee if we say the right words or use the right tone. The devil doesn't flee because we've fasted or paid our tithe or attended an all-night prayer meeting. Exerting our spirituality doesn't scare him. He flees because we have submitted ourselves to God. We have believed what He said about us is true. And we have stood in our rightful place of authority.

Beloved, spiritual authority is not tied to your personal power or holiness. It's tied to the position you hold as a child of God. It's about who you are in Christ. When God looks at you, what does He see? If you've been paying attention during this teaching, you know He sees Jesus. But do you know what the enemy sees when he looks at you? If you are a believer, he also sees Jesus.

In New Testament times, Rome had conquered most of the known world. The Roman military made a name for themselves by being ruthless in battle and thoroughly conquering their enemies. After overthrowing an enemy power, the Romans would capture the highest-ranking official and make an "open show" of him. They would chop off his thumbs so he could never again wield a sword. They'd cut off his big toes, so he could never run away. Then strip him naked, chain him to a cart, and parade him through the city streets. Citizens would throw rotten vegetables and stones at the prisoner; and as they marched, the Roman centurions would shout, "Look at your enemy! He is no threat to you!" By the time the Romans finished triumphing over their enemy, he was usually dead.

This is the practice Paul was alluding to when he wrote:

And you, being dead in your sins and the uncircumcision of your flesh, hath he quickened together with him, having forgiven you all trespasses; blotting out the handwriting of ordinances that was against us, which was contrary to us, and took it out of the way, nailing it to his cross; and having spoiled principalities and powers, he made a shew of them openly, triumphing over them in it (Colossians 2:13-15 KJV).

Jesus rendered our enemy defenseless when He triumphed over him in the cross. Jesus made an "open show" of the devil declaring, "Look at your enemy! He is no threat. Only believe!" Satan remembers that when he looks at you. He remembers his humiliation. That's why he fights so hard to keep us deceived and distracted from who we are in Christ. He doesn't want us knowing his true position—or ours. He needs our authority. He needs us to stay focused on the circumstances of our flesh so that he can steal our inheritance.

Remember, we are three-part beings—spirit, soul, and body (1 Thessalonians 5:23). And just as our spirit and soul have specific functions in life, so does our body. Our body is our position of authority in this world. And when we learn to recognize these spiritual truths choosing—with our mind, will, and emotions (our soul)—to trust in and declare the word, we awaken to our God-given authority and begin to see His Word manifest in our physical bodies. We are healthy, happy, and prosperous. We lay hands on the sick, and they recover. We raise the dead. We cast out demons and set captives free—just like Jesus did.

I remember a story about a missionary in Mexico named David Hogan. David is a man of great faith, and through his ministry he has seen over 500 people raised from the dead.[1] He said that while in a jungle village one time, he encountered a terrible smell. No matter how long he stayed in the village, the smell wouldn't dissipate. It just kept assaulting his senses. Finally David asked the local pastor about it. The pastor pointed to a pile of rags off to the side. David was overcome with curiosity so he walked toward the pile. The closer he got, the stronger the smell became. He reached out to pick the top rag off the pile and found a man decomposing with leprosy. The man was barely alive. He had no nose, no ears, no fingers. Every orifice was oozing pus, and as David began to walk away, the Lord said, "Preach! The Kingdom of Heaven is at hand."

David returned to the man and began telling him about Jesus. He led the man to the Lord, covered him back up, and stood to walk away. Again the Lord spoke, *"Heal the sick, cleanse the lepers, raise the dead, cast out demons. Freely you have received, freely give"* (Matthew 10:8).

All right, Lord, David thought. He took a deep breath and began to preach to the man. "I'm going to pray for you," he said after a few minutes. But the Holy Spirit spoke to his heart, *"Lay hands on the sick and they will recover."*

David reached out, placed his hand on the man's head—a man with contagious leprosy—and prayed, "Be healed and whole in Jesus' name!" David said his hand sunk into the man's flesh, but he determined to trust God's Word. He knew God would not ask him to do something that would harm him. So when he finished praying, David pulled his hand out of the man's skull, covered it, and told the pastor to get a bucket of water and lye soap.

As David washed his hands, doubt chanted through his mind, *You're going to die of leprosy. You're going to die of leprosy.* But he resisted the thought, finished washing his hands, and began preaching to the rest of the people. Many were saved during that trip, and when he returned several months later, a man approached him. David said he was a handsome, muscular man grinning from ear to ear. "Do I know you?" he asked.

"Yes, you know me," the man replied.

"I don't think I know you," David said. "I don't remember meeting you."

"You do know me," the man replied. "The last time you saw me, I had no fingers or nose. You prayed for me and I was healed!"

I'm telling you, nothing is impossible when we get a revelation of our spiritual authority! Yes, the enemy attacks. But his only real weapon in the believer's life is deception. Jesus stripped him of all else. Jesus led *"captivity captive"* (Ephesians 4:8) and set us free. We cannot, outside our own consent, be held captive any longer.

When we know how to discern between life and death, between the spirit and the flesh, between God's handiwork and the enemy's— we are unstoppable. The truths we learned in Sunday school move from sweet fairy tale and tradition to spiritual and physical reality. So the litmus test becomes what do *we* see when we look at ourselves? If you or I can't answer "Jesus," then we're missing a vital piece of our spiritual foundation and will find ourselves struggling against the enemy's attacks instead of overcoming.

Note

1. Rhoda Gayle, "David Hogan Recounts How His Ministry has Seen Over 500 People Raised from the Dead," *GodTV*, December 18, 2019; https://godtv.com/david-hogan-sid-roth/; accessed February 8, 2021.

13

Our Spiritual Authority

I once heard a story about a woman who was told she had cancer. She hadn't been feeling well and went to the doctor for some tests. When the doctor gave her the diagnosis he said, "It has spread throughout your entire body. I'm so sorry; there is nothing we can do. Go home. Spend the time with your family." The woman began laughing and the doctor, thinking she was in shock, said, "Ma'am, please. Calm down. We'll help in whatever way we can...just, please, calm down. Would you like me to call someone? Do you need a sedative?"

The woman, who was a believer, just kept laughing. She finally gathered herself and told the doctor to run the tests again. The doctor thought she was crazy, but to keep her calm he agreed to run the tests again. Two hours later, he returned. Sitting down and shaking his head, the doctor said, "I don't know what happened. But we can't find any signs of cancer in your body. We ran the tests multiple times and compared them to your old tests. There's nothing there. Tell me, what was that laughing thing you did?"

The woman looked at the doctor and said, "When the devil tells me a lie, I laugh" (see Psalm 37:12-13).

When Satan attacks, when circumstances slap us in the face, or somebody says something that goes against God's Word, we have a choice to make. Will we heed the enemy's lies, or will we respond in faith? Will we agree with God and submit to His Word? Will we resist the enemy? Will we take our thoughts and words captive to make them obey Christ (2 Corinthians 10:5)?

> *Be sober, be vigilant; because your adversary the devil walks about like a roaring lion, seeking whom he may devour* (1 Peter 5:8).

We must remain sober and vigilant. We cannot put down our guard. Our enemy is on the prowl looking for someone to devour, but it doesn't have to be us. In this verse, *sober* means sound-minded or self-controlled. It's the opposite of intoxicated. It means we have the right perspective; we're looking at and interpreting our circumstances properly. *Vigilant* means to be on guard, to be ready for whatever happens. A vigilant soldier stays in the proper position, ready for battle. And like a soldier, our response in the moment of attack determines the battle's outcome. We need to remain sober and vigilant. We need to judge our circumstances by the reality of God's Word, and remain on guard so that when the enemy roars, we respond correctly.

A lion's roar is a powerful sound meant to instill fear and command attention. We once visited a zoo in central Russia full of exotic animals, monkeys, and beautiful tigers; but when the lion roared, every eye in the place turned toward his exhibit. The same thing happens in the wild. In the wild, a lion's roar paralyzes prey and inspires the respect of its competition. Every animal knows the alpha lion's roar is backed by a powerful set of teeth and claws. Without them, the lion is nothing.

The alpha is the leader of a pride of lions. Though there may be three to five other males in a pride, there is only one alpha. All others are subservient him. The females hunt, but the alpha eats first. The young males help protect the pride, but the alpha gets first pick of the mates. Though another may come to challenge the alpha, his strength and experience expels the challenger and forces him out to manage the savanna alone.

Scripture calls Jesus the *"Lion of the tribe of Judah"* (Revelation 5:5). Though Satan tried to challenge our Lord, he failed miserably! He may still roar, but there is no substance to his roaring, no claws or teeth to back up his boast. So we must keep his roaring in its proper perspective and not allow fear to carry us away. We must remain sober. And Scripture says as we do these things our enemy will flee (James 4:7; Malachi 3:11).

A creek runs on the property where we used to live. The water was only about two feet deep, but at certain times of the year, it rushed through our property like the bona fide mountain stream it was. If a ball fell in, the kids would race it downstream to catch it before the ball disappeared past the bridges. When we started teaching our kids about their spiritual authority, we'd use that creek to help them visualize the power of their words. If they were sick, we prayed then said, "Sickness, we rebuke you in Jesus' name and throw you into the river!" It helped them understand that when we rebuke the enemy, he has to go—quickly! (Like all kids, though, they took it a step further. They'd say, "No Momma, tell him it's a river of lava." They weren't willing to wait for him to flee; they wanted him burnt up on impact!)

One winter, our daughter had a persistent sore throat. We rebuked it, and Ellie would start to feel better and run off to play. Then, a bit later she'd come back with her throat still hurting. So we'd pray again. Again, her throat would feel better and she'd run off to play. Back and forth all day. Pray and play; pray and play. Ellie understood that the devil had to leave when we prayed, so every time we prayed she experienced healing. But it began to bother her that the sore throat kept coming back. "Momma," she asked, "why is it that when we pray, I get healed, but then the devil comes back?"

I wasn't sure how to answer that. All I could think to say was, "Because he's stupid." And he is. But the devil is also persistent. He'll keep roaring to instill fear and doubt hoping that we will eventually grow weary and put down your guard. He will roar "lack." He will roar "sickness." He will roar "fear." But remember that his roaring has no substance. It is our response that determines whether or not we're consumed.

Our adversary only walks about *"like a roaring lion."* He has no real power. He is not our Lion. He is *"seeking whom he **may** devour."* The enemy can't devour everyone. He roars, but he has no teeth. He may still try to exert force over the pride, roaring to inspire fear, but he is not the alpha male. He can only devour those who yield to his threats. So what do you do when a lion roars? You roar right back! You roar the Word of God. You roar as a representative of God—the true Lion—and watch all imposters flee.

Throughout the Gospels we read that the people marveled at Jesus' sayings because *"He taught them as one having authority,"* not as their scribes and teachers of the law (Mark 1:22; Matthew 7:28, 13:54; Luke 2:47, 4:32). Jesus exuded authority because He knew who He was. He knew Who He was representing. When the soldiers came to take Jesus away, He told His disciples to put away their swords, *"Do you think that I cannot now pray to My Father, and He will provide Me with more than twelve legions of angels?"* (Matthew 26:53). Jesus didn't have to see into the supernatural to know He had access to it. He didn't have to pray about His Father's will. He didn't question what was happening to Him. He knew the Word, and He knew the authority in which He walked.

Jesus operated in absolute power under perfect control. He was the meekest Man on the face of the earth. We often associate meekness with weakness, but it is quite the opposite. Jesus didn't operate in fear. He wasn't intimidated by the religious leaders. He preached the Kingdom boldly. He did not mince words with the Pharisees. No matter what happened to Him—when He was threatened, when the people wanted to stone Him, when they mocked and whipped Him, even when they nailed Him to the cross—Jesus maintained self-control. He knew His authority.

At any point during His trial and crucifixion, Jesus could have called every angel in Heaven to rescue Him. He didn't deserve the cross. He didn't relish the pain. But He knew the joy His obedience would reap; Jesus saw the future harvest (Hebrews 12:2) and kept His circumstances in their proper perspective.

We need to keep our circumstances in their proper, eternal perspective as well. Too often we forget our spiritual position and the authority that comes with that position. We may not be presidents or high-ranking CEOs, but we are children of the King. We are royalty. And we need to learn to live as who we are.

We cannot get offended by what people do or say. Their words have no authority in our lives; they do not define who we are. Still we take them personally. Can their words or actions dictate our future? No. So why do we allow them to dominate our thoughts and drain our mental energy? Why do we allow them to direct our choices? They are not our Alpha. We must learn to *"Resist...steadfast in the faith, knowing that the same sufferings are experienced by your brotherhood in the world"* (1 Peter 5:9). For, *"...the God of all grace, who called us to His eternal glory by Christ Jesus, after you have suffered a while, perfect, establish, strengthen, and settle you"* (1 Peter 5:10).

We are not alone in our fight of faith. God has not left us as orphans. The same Spirit who lived in Jesus lives in us. The same authority and self-control He walked in, we can walk in. God is not withholding anything from us. We are His image bearers. We were built to overcome.

Everything we see in the Word is our inheritance. But we have to renew our minds to it. We have to remove all our self- or others-imposed limits and begin to see ourselves the way He sees us. His nature lives in us. His ability, His righteousness, His power, His peace—it's all there. We have everything we need to do everything He has called us to do (Hebrews 13:21).

Grace and peace be multiplied to you in the knowledge of God and of Jesus our Lord, as His divine power has given to us all things that pertain to life and godliness, through the knowledge of Him who called us by glory and virtue, by which have been given to us exceedingly great and precious promises, that through these you may be partakers of the divine nature... (2 Peter 1:2-4).

We are *"partakers of the divine nature"* and joint heirs with Christ (Romans 8:17). We have a share in His inheritance (Colossians 1:12) because Jesus made us *"more than conquerors"* (Romans 8:37).

A visiting minister once told us of a prizefighter in the championship ring. This boxer has dedicated his whole life to training for the championship. Every practice, every winning fight brought him one step closer to the title. But in the process, he also got bloodied, broke his nose, and had to get stitches. Each time, his trainer encouraged him, "You can do this. You've trained for this. You're a conqueror. You can be the champion." So the fighter kept going out there. He kept winning and making a name for himself conquering every opponent they threw in the ring with him.

Finally, the boxer made it to the championship bout. When the referee called him and his opponent into the center of the ring, he realized this was going to be the fight of his life. In that moment, he saw an opponent who'd also been training and fighting his way to the top. He saw the scars on his opponent's face, and he knew the price he paid to get there. In the center, the referee read over the rules and *Ding!* the bell signaled the first round.

The two men danced around and exchanged a few blows look-ing for their opponent's weaknesses. Punch! Dodge. Sidestep. Fake. Punch! Each man getting knocked back and returning for more—round after round. Finally, in the fifth round, our challenger came in close. He got his opponent on the ropes and delivered the knock-out blow. Boom! The opponent was down for the count. "One," the referee shouted. "Two!...Three!...Eight!...Nine!...Ten!" Our challenger was the new heavyweight-boxing champion of the world! He got the belt. He got the fame. He got the jewelry and the prize money, and he knew the pain was worth it. The blood, sweat, and tears were only down payments. He had conquered. He was the champion!

But as they ushered him out of the ring and into the locker room, his girl looked him in the face and held out her hand. She smiled at him and he handed it all over to her. In that moment, she became "more than a conqueror." She didn't have to train for that money. She never got sweaty. She didn't fight or bleed for it. But she did receive the reward! And that's exactly what Jesus did for us.

> *Surely He has borne our griefs and carried our sorrows;*
> *yet we esteemed Him stricken, smitten by God, and*
> *afflicted. But He was wounded for our transgressions,*
> *He was bruised for our iniquities; the chastisement for*
> *our peace was upon Him, and by His stripes we are*
> *healed* (Isaiah 53:4-5 NLT).

Jesus suffered through all the training, He took the bruises and endured the fight so we could become more than conquerors. Now we stand in His position—not just in our spirit, it starts there but it is meant to work its way out through our spirit, soul, and body. We have been restored to the place God created Adam to have, given the authority He intended Adam to keep. And though there is an enemy, the enemy has no teeth.

When we walk in the Spirit, we will experience the victory Jesus died to give; and like Paul, we can say, *"I have fought the good fight, I have finished the race, I have kept the faith"* (2 Timothy 4:7).

14

The Grace to Minister

Each of these foundational principles are meant to impact three areas of your life: (1) your personal relationship with God; (2) the way you respond to difficult life circumstances and enemy attacks; and (3) the way you minister to others. When you know how much God loves you, it opens the door to relationship with Him. You realize that God made you in His image. He sees you different from the way you see yourself, and it prompts you to recognize your identity as a *new creature in Christ Jesus* (2 Corinthians 5:17).

You are encouraged to live and walk after the Spirit (Galatians 5:25). Knowing both who you are and who God is in you causes you to respond righteously to life's circumstances. You understand God's true nature; you recognize the enemy's tactics and are empowered to step into your spiritual authority so you can resist the enemy and minister to others out of the same grace you have been given (Matthew 10:8).

The Spirit of God within us can do *"exceedingly, abundantly above all we can ask or think,"* or as some translations say, "imagine" (Ephesians 3:20). And we've only scratched the surface of His character.

God loves us. He wants to outdo our thoughts and take us places we've never dreamed. He wants to answer our prayers and use us to change the world. Allow God's Word to reignite your hopes and passions. Allow the Scriptures to change your mind. If you have questions, the Bible holds the answers. But we must keep growing in each of these life foundations. We must incorporate them into our relationship with God. We have to move from knowledge, which puffs up, to revelation, which builds up and prompts change.

Many Scriptures reinforce the principles we have been discussing—most of which are cited in the Appendix. One of our favorites is found in John 14:12. Jesus said, *"Most assuredly, I say to you, he who believes in Me, the works that I do he will do also; and greater works than these he will do, because I go to My Father."* That's amazing! We can do the *"greater works"* of Jesus because His Spirit lives in us. We are able because He is able. His Spirit has already healed the sick and raised the dead. So His Spirit joined with our spirit can too.

His Spirit has already cleansed the leper and cast out demons. So His Spirit joined with our spirit can too, for the Scriptures say, *"He who is joined to the Lord is one spirit with Him"* (1 Corinthians 6:17). This world, and all its problems, will pass away. But God's Word and our relationship with Him will last forever. So will all we accomplish in cooperation with His Spirit. What joy it will be when we stand before the Father and hear, *"Well done, good and faithful servant... Enter into the joy of your lord"* (Matthew 25:21,23). But until then, let's keep growing. Let's keep believing. And let's keep acting on our faith.

Faith is how we please God (Hebrews 11:6). When we get to Heaven, we won't need faith. We will see God face to face. We will walk and talk with Him. Our desires will be instantly met. We won't need faith in Heaven, so let's walk in faith now. Let's please God now. Let's enjoy being stretched. Let's remember who lives inside us. Remember what He has called us to and believe His Word. Let's grow in our understanding of authority.

Then, when problems and circumstances hit us in the face, we can laugh. We know the devil has no authority in our life. We belong to God. And we have been called to greater works. We can see our finances recover. We can see our families saved. We can see our neighbors healed. We can see our children thrive. Psalm 21:2 says that God gives us the desires of our heart. He does not withhold the request of our lips. Let's trust that truth.

My pastor used to say that within every believer's heart is a throne and a cross. Jesus is on one, you are on the other. Which one are you on? Are you on the throne, or are you on the cross? Growing in *Life Foundations* will encourage you to take your proper position. It will empower you to step off the throne and onto the cross—to truly make Jesus the Lord and leader of your life. There is no need to fear. God's will toward you is good. He will take you places you never dreamed of going. And you will be able to minister to others, regardless of the circumstance.

Too many times believers think *I'd love to minister, but I'm not qualified. I don't know Greek. I don't have a testimony...so I'll just stay in the background.* No! We need you! You are a unique part of the body of Christ (1 Corinthians 12:27). Each of us has a unique relationship with the Lord. We have unique testimonies, unique insight based on His Word. Though we are all created in His image, there is no one exactly like you or exactly like me. So we shouldn't expect God to use us or speak to us in the same way. There's a grace on your life—a gifting—no one else has. You can go places and reach people no one else can. We're not in competition with one another. We part of a team.

> There are diversities of gifts, but the same Spirit. There are differences of ministries, but the same Lord. And there are diversities of activities, but it is the same God who works all in all. But the manifestation of the Spirit is given to each one for the profit of all (1 Corinthians 12:4-7).

You are not insignificant! God's Kingdom advances when you advance. Don't be intimidated. Don't dismiss God's Spirit within you. Learn to minister out of these six principles—*Life Foundations.* Every issue of life, every scriptural principle fits into one of these foundations. We've used these truths to minister for more than fifteen years. We've used them to teach teenagers and Bible school students. We've used them to encourage pastors, to counsel families, to instruct singles. We've used them in the United States, in Russia, and in our own home. They apply to everything! They work everywhere.

When we taught these truths to teenagers, we made it fun. We played games, blared music, and shared our testimonies. We taught them how much God loved them. We showed them how to stay out of sin. We encouraged them to submit to their parents—and it wasn't exactly a captive audience. Most didn't want to be there. They were dragged out of bed at 7:30 in the morning to spend a week of their summer listening to someone preach at them.

We started out saying, "We know your year hasn't been great. You've been watching things, doing things you're not proud of. You got involved with stuff you don't want your parents to know about. You're hiding things on your phone. You've been having sex. You've started doing drugs. Some of you have been bullied. Others have been raped and you haven't told anybody. You're even considering suicide. But God loves you. Those things are not who you are. Those things are not what He sees."

The tears would start rolling down their faces and then we taught them *Life Foundations*. By Thursday night, 80 to 90 percent of those teenagers had rededicated their lives to the Lord. They told us, "For the first time in my life, I know God loves me…I don't have to prove anything to God…I have authority over sin…Now I understand that bad choices don't define me. God's Spirit lives in me and I have a destiny."

We also shared these truths at a drug rehab center in Russia. Men entered the center broken and hurting, emaciated and dirty. They didn't need to be lectured about their addictions. They knew they had a problem. They didn't need facts about heroin and alcohol abuse. They knew they were at rock bottom. So we took them to God's Word. We shared these foundational truths of God's love and acceptance, and their inherent worth in His sight. We told them that God had a plan for their life. That He was willing to walk with them through the mess and pain their addiction had created. And that only He could transform their lives from the inside out and bring them to a place of recovery.

In the months we were there, it was amazing to watch those hopeless men become powerhouses for the Kingdom. They began sharing their testimonies and talking about Jesus with everyone they met. It was incredible!

You can do the same exact thing. It doesn't matter who you are. It doesn't matter where you're from or what culture you're speaking into; God's Word is the same. It crosses borders and connects languages. It stirs up faith.

Share these foundations. Show others God's true nature. Teach them about their new identity in Christ. Remember what the revelation of God's love did in your life, and give someone else the chance to receive it.

When we did this at the drug rehab center, the results were phenomenal. For years the center tried to power people through the recovery process by making them earn "discipleship points." The men read. They prayed. They memorized Scripture and worked some menial task. Everything they did was to meet the requirements of the program and "earn" the privilege of staying at the center. But there was no heart change. So when the men "graduated," they fell back into drugs. They needed more than "points." They needed Grace.

Grace is about relationship with God. It's not a checklist. Giving people a to-do list doesn't work. Pointing out their failures doesn't work either. Reading the Word, praying, and memorizing Scripture are all good things. But the goal of those disciplines is relationship with God the Father. The motivation for them is grace. When people understand how much God loves them, how much He has done for them, and how He wants to bless them, it changes their hearts. And that change drives habit change.

You can't change anyone. Neither can I. That's why we don't base ministry on our experiences or personality. We don't have to have a like testimony to minister to drug addicts. We don't need a special gifting to reach prostitutes or prison convicts. Ministry is an overflow of relationship with God. It manifests itself in different ways, but it's all built on the foundation of grace. Some ministry happens from behind a pulpit, some from behind a desk. Some ministry happens on the streets and some around the dinner table.

God has given each of us the authority and responsibility to take His gospel and share His life everywhere we go. Paul wrote, *"The things which you learned and received and heard and saw in me, these do, and the God of peace will be with you"* (Philippians 4:9). In other words, be an example. Let others see the life of God in you. Let them see how you love your spouse, how you deal with your children. Let them see how you handle your finances, what you do in crisis, how you extend forgiveness. That's what being a minister is. Don't worry about being perfect, just stay humble and surrendered to God. Let others see the Word work; let them see the grace of God in action so they have an example to follow (1 Timothy 4:12).

God's Word holds the answer to every human problem, every societal issue. Its truth is not relative to your circumstances. It's not based on experience. It's based on the principles—the unchangeable law and nature—of God. Everything we need is found in the Bible. In ministry, you may run into people who are confused about the Word, who are struggling with depression or need help in their marriages.

They say things like, "I believe God loves me. I'm praying in Jesus' name, but nothing happens. Maybe this is just a cross I have to bear. Maybe God is trying to teach me something." They have believed a lie. They have allowed their circumstances to trump God's Word. But God's Word is greater than our circumstances. It's higher than our thoughts or emotions (Isaiah 55:9). And it applies to everyone. Everyone is equal at the foot of the cross.

Life Foundations connects the basic principles of the Word together. It shows people how God's Word as recorded in the Scriptures applies to their lives. People going through depression don't need to hear they are weak and faithless. They need to understand how much God loves them, how He sees them. A person constantly offended needs to learn how to walk in the spirit and see others by the spirit. Someone struggling with finances needs to know that Jehovah Jireh lives in them.

People struggling with their marriages need to know they are complete in Christ. They need to stop expecting something out of their mate that their mate was never intended to be. Marriage is not a "you complete me" type relationship. Marriage is one person—complete in Christ—finding another person—complete in Christ—to walk through life beside. But belittling these people for their lack of understanding or trying to force them into the grace of God is wrong. *Life Foundations* is not meant to bulldoze people's faith. People are where they are, and they move forward by revelation. That's why we share God's grace with others first through our way of life.

Then, as they see the difference between our life—which is a reflection of God's life—and theirs, the way is opened for us to communicate the truth with them. *"So then faith comes by hearing, and hearing by the word of God"* (Romans 10:17).

Notice how you have to keep hearing the word for it to produce faith in your life. But this process is not just for you. It's awesome that you're being transformed. It's awesome that you're being healed, that you're walking out of depression—but the principles you learn from *Life Foundations* are meant for more than that. They are for the people in your sphere of influence.

When you begin to live your life by these principles, not just by your circumstances, you become a walking billboard for the Lord. You become the answer to someone's prayer. The world needs you to be an example of God's grace, an example of His love. You may be the only Jesus they see. But as you grow, remember where you came from.

Remember that the people you're ministering to are where you once were. Be gracious to them. Lead them back to the Bible. Show them who God is. Teach them to walk in the victory these foundational principles of God's Word have laid. And then watch as the atmosphere around you changes for the better!

Conclusion

The foundational truths of God's Word fuel our growth and empower us to overcome life's challenges. First John 4:17 says in part, *"As He is, so are we in this world."* We don't have to wait for Heaven to be like Jesus. The same Spirit who lived in Jesus lives in us. That truth is so powerful! But that's not all that passage of Scripture says. Let's look at the verses surrounding verse 17:

> *And we have known and believed the love that God has for us. God is love, and he who abides in love abides in God, and God in him. Love has been perfected among us in this: that we may have boldness in the day of judgment; because as He is, so are we in this world. There is no fear in love; but perfect love casts out fear, because fear involves torment. But he who fears has not been made perfect in love* (1 John 4:16-18).

God's love gives us confidence—confidence in the *"day of judgement"* and confidence in this world. We're not victims. We're victors! We're not fearful in the face of challenging circumstances. God's love frees us from fear. It frees us from a fear of judgment and failure, the fear of people, the fear of disappointment. God's love fuels our faith and revolutionizes the way we live. It is the cornerstone of every other spiritual foundation. We're no longer afraid of angering a temperamental God. We're not afraid of an enemy attack. Love gives us a proper perspective of the future.

> So when this corruptible has put on incorruption, and this mortal has put on immortality, then shall be brought to pass the saying that is written: "Death is swallowed up in victory." "O Death, where is your sting? O Hades, where is your victory?" The sting of death is sin, and the strength of sin is the law. But thanks be to God, who gives us the victory through our Lord Jesus Christ (1 Corinthians 15:54-57).

Jesus broke the power of fear and death in our lives. He took away its sting. We don't have to fear dying; we don't have to fear disease or suffering. We can live life to the fullest. What's the worst that can happen? Going to be with the Lord? That is joy! *"So we say with confidence, 'The Lord is my helper; I will not be afraid. What can mere mortals do to me?'"* (Hebrews 13:6 NIV).

We pray *Life Foundations* has equipped you to *"take up the shield of faith, with which you can extinguish all the flaming arrows of the evil one"* (Ephesians 6:16 NIV). That it has reminded you of who you are, and shown you God's true nature. We pray it has reignited your personal relationship with God and empowered you to resist the enemy and walk in your spiritual authority. That it has reminded you of all Christ accomplished on your behalf and placed within you as a guarantee (2 Corinthians 5:5).

And we also pray *Life Foundations* has challenged you to leave your comfort zone and begin ministering to others. Jesus said, *"All authority in heaven and on earth has been given to me. Therefore go..."* (Matthew 28:18 NIV). The truths presented in *Life Foundations* are not just for us to receive. They are also for us to give (Matthew 10:8). It's our job to now take what Jesus did and share His victory with the world. And we don't need a seminary degree to do that. We don't have to read Greek or Hebrew. We have the power we need to make Him known.

Because God loves me, I can _____ (fill in the rest of the sentence: be healed, have peace, overcome addiction, be prosperous—whatever it is you can now do because of God's love).

We know God didn't give us trials to teach us anything. That's not His nature. The enemy may be trying to steal from us. He may be trying to twist our understanding of God's love. But Christ lives in us. We lack no good thing. Our victory is a finished work. Now we get to choose. Are we going to see ourselves the way God sees us? Are we going to believe His Word above our circumstances? Are we going to stand in our authority knowing that our enemy is a defeated foe? Will we choose to overcome and share these truths with others?

Demonstrating God's love through Christlike compassion is Jesus' definition of ministry. In Matthew 10:7-8, Jesus told His disciples to, *"...go, preach, saying, 'The kingdom of heaven is at hand.' Heal the sick, cleanse the lepers, raise the dead, cast out demons. Freely you have received, freely give."* But this type of ministry only comes as an overflow of our relationship with God. We can't give what we don't have. We can't share what we don't know. That's why *Life Foundations* is so important. But as we've said before, these principles are not one-time revelations. They are part of our spiritual journey—part of a growing relationship with God. The deeper we go into the Scriptures contained in the Bible, the more we dig into these truths, the more impactful they become.

We guarantee that as you search out these principles, meditating on them and asking the Holy Spirit to teach you, your relationship with God will transform. You will overcome fear. You will overcome life's circumstances. You will be able to resist the enemy and minister to others—no matter what they've experienced in life.

Every time we have ministered on *Life Foundations*—in literally dozens of nations now—it has transformed us. It has brought us intimacy with the Father and more grace in our relationships with others. Each time we study these principles, the Holy Spirit sparks new understandings and deeper insights within us. And we know He will do the same for you.

Enjoy the journey!

> *Father, You are for us and there is nothing and no one who can stand against us. We thank You for walking us through this process of transformation. We know, according to Jeremiah 31:3, that You have loved us with an everlasting love and that with Your lovingkindness, You draw us.*
>
> *Thank You for giving us Your Spirit, for teaching us to*

walk after the Spirit and into our God-given authority. We choose to use Your Word like a mirror to see who we really are and how You want us to live. Thank You for pulling us out of our comfort zones and calling us to greater things than we ever thought possible.

Help us to grow in these truths, to remain teachable so we can declare Your goodness to this generation. Thank You for being such a good God, for revealing Yourself to us through Your Word. We love You and commit our lives to You. You are faithful. We refute the enemy and thank You for equipping us to do Your will. In Jesus' name and because of His finished work, we pray these things boldly, knowing You hear us. Amen.

Life Foundations Scriptures

God's Word is vital to our understanding of who He is and who He made us to be. While we haven't cited each and every Scripture that has ministered these truths to us, we encourage you to use the following passages from the Bible as jumping-off points in your study. We pray you will continue building your life on the solidity of God's Word.

Life FOUNDATION:
THE LOVE OF GOD

But God, who is rich in mercy, because of His great love with which He loved us, even when we were dead in trespasses, made us alive together with Christ (by grace you have been saved), and raised us up together, and made us sit together in the heavenly places in Christ Jesus, that in the ages to come He might show the exceeding riches of His grace in His kindness toward us in Christ Jesus. For by grace you have been saved through faith, and that not of yourselves; it is the gift of God, not of works, lest anyone should boast. For we are His workmanship, created in Christ Jesus for good works, which God prepared beforehand that we should walk in them (Ephesians 2:4-10).

And walk in love, as Christ also has loved us and given Himself for us, an offering and a sacrifice to God for a sweet-smelling aroma (Ephesians 5:2).

But when the kindness and love of God our Savior appeared, he saved us, not because of righteous things we had done, but because of his mercy. He saved us through the washing of rebirth and renewal by the Holy Spirit, whom he poured out on us generously through Jesus Christ our Savior, so that, having been justified by his grace, we might become heirs having the hope of eternal life (Titus 3:4-7 NIV).

Behold what manner of love the Father has bestowed on us, that we should be called children of God! Therefore the world does not know us, because it did not know Him. Beloved, now we are children of God; and it has not yet been revealed what we shall be, but we know that when He is revealed, we shall be like Him, for we shall see Him as He is (1 John 3:1-2).

Beloved, let us love one another, for love is of God; and everyone who loves is born of God and knows God. He who does not love does not know God, for God is love. In this the love of God was manifested toward us, that God has sent His only begotten Son into the world, that we might live through Him. In this is love, not that we loved God, but that He loved us and sent His Son to be the propitiation for our sins. Beloved, if God so loved us, we also ought to love one another (1 John 4:7-11).

And we have known and believed the love that God has for us. God is love, and he who abides in love abides in God, and God in him. Love has been perfected among us in this: that we may have boldness in the day of judgment; because as He is, so are we in this world. There is no fear in love; but perfect love casts out fear, because fear involves torment. But he who fears has not been made perfect in love. We love Him because He first loved us (1 John 4:16-19).

The Lord your God in your midst, The Mighty One, will save; He will rejoice over you with gladness, He will quiet you with His love, He will rejoice over you with singing (Zephaniah 3:17).

Yet in all these things we are more than conquerors through Him who loved us (Romans 8:37).

He brought me to the banqueting house, and his banner over me was love (Song of Solomon 2:4).

Fear not, for I am with you; be not dismayed, for I am your God. I will strengthen you, yes, I will help you, I will uphold you with My righteous right hand (Isaiah 41:10).

Life FOUNDATION:
SPIRT, SOUL, AND BODY

But as many as received Him, to them He gave the right to become children of God, to those who believe in His name: who were born, not of blood, nor of the will of the flesh, nor of the will of man, but of God (John 1:12-13).

For those who live according to the flesh set their minds on the things of the flesh, but those who live according to the Spirit, the things of the Spirit. For to be carnally minded is death, but to be spiritually minded is life and peace (Romans 8:5-6).

But you are not in the flesh but in the Spirit, if indeed the Spirit of God dwells in you. Now if anyone does not have the Spirit of Christ, he is not His. And if Christ is in you, the body is dead because of sin, but the Spirit is life because of righteousness. But if the Spirit of Him who raised Jesus from the dead dwells in you, He who raised Christ from the dead will also give life to your mortal bodies through His Spirit who dwells in you (Romans 8:9-11).

The Spirit Himself bears witness with our spirit that we are children of God (Romans 8:16).

But of Him you are in Christ Jesus, who became for us wisdom from God—and righteousness and sanctification and redemption (1 Corinthians 1:30).

These are the things God has revealed to us by his Spirit. The Spirit searches all things, even the deep things of God. For who knows a person's thoughts except their own spirit within them? In the same way no one knows the thoughts of God except the Spirit of

God. What we have received is not the spirit of the world, but the Spirit who is from God, so that we may understand what God has freely given us. This is what we speak, not in words taught us by human wisdom but in words taught by the Spirit, explaining spiritual realities with Spirit-taught words. The person without the Spirit does not accept the things that come from the Spirit of God but considers them foolishness, and cannot understand them because they are discerned only through the Spirit. The person with the Spirit makes judgments about all things, but such a person is not subject to merely human judgments, for, "Who has known the mind of the Lord so as to instruct him?" But we have the mind of Christ (1 Corinthians 2:10-16 NIV).

Do you not know that you are the temple of God and that the Spirit of God dwells in you? (1 Corinthians 3:16)

But whoever is united with the Lord is one with him in spirit (1 Corinthians 6:17 NIV).

Love has been perfected among us in this: that we may have boldness in the day of judgment; because as He is, so are we in this world (1 John 4:17).

And you, being dead in your trespasses and the uncircumcision of your flesh, He has made alive together with Him, having forgiven you all trespasses, having wiped out the handwriting of requirements that was against us, which was contrary to us. And He has taken it out of the way, having nailed it to the cross (Colossians 2:13-14).

Life FOUNDATION:
HOW GOD SEES US

But the Lord said to Samuel, "Do not look at his appearance or at his physical stature, because I have refused him. For the Lord does not see as man sees; for man looks at the outward appearance, but the Lord looks at the heart" (1 Samuel 16:7).

For if by the one man's offense death reigned through the one, much more those who receive abundance of grace and of the gift of righteousness will reign in life through the One, Jesus Christ (Romans 5:17).

Therefore, if anyone is in Christ, he is a new creation; old things have passed away; behold, all things have become new (2 Corinthians 5:17).

In Him you also trusted, after you heard the word of truth, the gospel of your salvation; in whom also, having believed, you were sealed with the Holy Spirit of promise (Ephesians 1:13).

But God, who is rich in mercy, because of His great love with which He loved us, even when we were dead in trespasses, made us alive together with Christ (by grace you have been saved), and raised us up together, and made us sit together in the heavenly places in Christ Jesus, that in the ages to come He might show the exceeding riches of His grace in His kindness toward us in Christ Jesus. For by grace you have been saved through faith, and that not of yourselves; it is the gift of God, not of works, lest anyone should boast. For we are His workmanship, created in Christ Jesus for good works, which God prepared beforehand that we should walk in them (Ephesians 2:4-10).

The mystery [of the gospel] which has been hidden from ages and from generations, but now has been revealed to His saints. To them God willed to make known what are the riches of the glory of this mystery among the Gentiles: which is Christ in you, the hope of glory (Colossians 1:26-27).

And you, being dead in your trespasses and the uncircumcision of your flesh, He has made alive together with Him, having forgiven you all trespasses (Colossians 2:13).

His divine power has given to us all things that pertain to life and godliness, through the knowledge of Him who called us by glory and virtue, by which have been given to us exceedingly great and precious promises, that through these you may be partakers of the divine nature, having escaped the corruption that is in the world through lust (2 Peter 1:3-4).

My little children, these things I write to you, so that you may not sin. And if anyone sins, we have an Advocate with the Father, Jesus Christ the righteous (1 John 2:1).

Life FOUNDATION:
IDENTITY IN CHRIST

For you did not receive the spirit of bondage again to fear, but you received the Spirit of adoption by whom we cry out, "Abba, Father." The Spirit Himself bears witness with our spirit that we are children of God, and if children, then heirs—heirs of God and joint heirs with Christ, if indeed we suffer with Him, that we may also be glorified together (Romans 8:15-17).

Yet in all these things we are more than conquerors through Him who loved us (Romans 8:37).

...put on the new self, created to be like God in true righteousness and holiness (Ephesians 4:24 NIV).

In Him also we have obtained an inheritance, being predestined according to the purpose of Him who works all things according to the counsel of His will (Ephesians 1:11).

For whom He foreknew, He also predestined to be conformed to the image of His Son, that He might be the firstborn among many brethren. Moreover whom He predestined, these He also called; whom He called, these He also justified; and whom He justified, these He also glorified (Romans 8:29-30).

But the fruit of the Spirit is love, joy, peace, longsuffering, kindness, goodness, faithfulness, gentleness, self-control. Against such there is no law. And those who are Christ's have crucified the flesh with its passions and desires. If we live in the Spirit, let us also walk in the Spirit (Galatians 5:22-25).

But God forbid that I should boast except in the cross of our Lord Jesus Christ, by whom the world has been crucified to me, and I to the world (Galatians 6:14).

But what things were gain to me, these I have counted loss for Christ. Yet indeed I also count all things loss for the excellence of the knowledge of Christ Jesus my Lord, for whom I have suffered the loss of all things, and count them as rubbish, that I may gain Christ and be found in Him, not having my own righteousness, which is from the law, but that which is through faith in Christ, the righteousness which is from God by faith; that I may know Him and the power of His resurrection, and the fellowship of His sufferings, being conformed to His death (Philippians 3:7-10).

For if by the one man's offense death reigned through the one, much more those who receive abundance of grace and of the gift of righteousness will reign in life through the One, Jesus Christ (Romans 5:17).

What shall we say then? Shall we continue in sin that grace may abound? Certainly not! How shall we who died to sin live any longer in it? Or do you not know that as many of us as were baptized into Christ Jesus were baptized into His death? Therefore we were buried with Him through baptism into death, that just as Christ was raised from the dead by the glory of the Father, even so we also should walk in newness of life. For if we have been united together in the likeness of His death, certainly we also shall be in the likeness of His resurrection, knowing this, that our old man was crucified with Him, that the body of sin might be done away with, that we should no longer be slaves of sin (Romans 6:1-6).

Life FOUNDATION:
THE TRUE NATURE OF GOD

Therefore know that the Lord your God, He is God, the faithful God who keeps covenant and mercy for a thousand generations with those who love Him and keep His commandments (Deuteronomy 7:9).

This is what the Lord says: "Let not the wise boast of their wisdom or the strong boast of their strength or the rich boast of their riches, but let the one who boasts boast about this: that they have the understanding to know me, that I am the Lord, who exercises kindness, justice and righteousness on earth, for in these I delight," declares the Lord* (Jeremiah 9:23-24 NIV).

For I will set My eyes on them for good, and I will bring them back to this land; I will build them and not pull them down, and I will plant them and not pluck them up. Then I will give them a heart to know Me, that I am the Lord; and they shall be My people, and I will be their God, for they shall return to Me with their whole heart (Jeremiah 24:6-7).

In the beginning was the Word, and the Word was with God, and the Word was God. ... And the Word became flesh and dwelt among us, and we beheld His glory, the glory as of the only begotten of the Father, full of grace and truth (John 1:1,14).

Jesus said to him, "Have I been with you so long, and yet you have not known Me, Philip? He who has seen Me has seen the Father; so how can you say, 'Show us the Father'? Do you not believe that I am in the Father, and the Father in Me? The words that I speak to you I do not speak on My own authority; but the Father who dwells in Me does the works" (John 14:9-10).

But God demonstrates His own love toward us, in that while we were still sinners, Christ died for us (Romans 5:8).

For He [God] made Him [Jesus] who knew no sin to be sin for us, that we might become the righteousness of God in Him (2 Corinthians 5:21).

To the praise of the glory of His grace, by which He made us accepted in the Beloved. In Him we have redemption through His blood, the forgiveness of sins, according to the riches of His grace (Ephesians 1:6-7).

God, who at various times and in various ways spoke in time past to the fathers by the prophets, has in these last days spoken to us by His Son, whom He has appointed heir of all things, through whom also He made the worlds; who being the brightness of His glory and the express image of His person, and upholding all things by the word of His power, when He had by Himself purged our sins, sat down at the right hand of the Majesty on high, having become so much better than the angels, as He has by inheritance obtained a more excellent name than they (Hebrews 1:1-4).

The Lord is not slack concerning His promise, as some count slackness, but is longsuffering toward us, not willing that any should perish but that all should come to repentance (2 Peter 3:9).

Life FOUNDATION:
BELIEVER'S AUTHORITY

For though we walk in the flesh, we do not war according to the flesh. For the weapons of our warfare are not carnal but mighty in God for pulling down strong-holds, casting down arguments and every high thing that exalts itself against the knowledge of God, bringing every thought into captivity to the obedience of Christ, and being ready to punish all disobedience when your obedience is fulfilled (2 Corinthians 10:3-6).

Then God blessed them, and God said to them, "Be fruitful and multiply; fill the earth and subdue it; have dominion over the fish of the sea, over the birds of the air, and over every living thing that moves on the earth" (Genesis 1:28).

Whoever believes and is baptized will be saved, but whoever does not believe will be condemned. And these signs will accompany those who believe: In my name they will drive out demons; they will speak in new tongues; they will pick up snakes with their hands; and when they drink deadly poison, it will not hurt them at all; they will place their hands on sick people, and they will get well (Mark 16:16-18 NIV).

Behold, I give you the authority to trample on serpents and scorpions, and over all the power of the enemy, and nothing shall by any means hurt you (Luke 10:19).

So I say to you: Ask and it will be given to you; seek and you will find; knock and the door will be opened to you. For everyone who asks receives; the one who seeks finds; and to the one who knocks, the door will be opened (Luke 11:9-10 NIV).

I can do all things through Christ who strengthens me (Philippians 4:13).

Therefore submit to God. Resist the devil and he will flee from you (James 4:7).

Therefore confess your sins to each other and pray for each other so that you may be healed. The prayer of a righteous person is powerful and effective (James 5:16 NIV).

For God has not given us a spirit of fear, but of power and of love and of a sound mind (2 Timothy 1:7).

Having disarmed principalities and powers, He made a public spectacle of them, triumphing over them in it (Colossians 2:15).

Additional Resources

We'd love to hear how *Life Foundations* has touched your life. Contact us at awmi.net. And keep growing in these truths by checking out the following resources:

Life Foundations Bible Buddy: Spur your growth by discovering hundreds of additional scriptures illuminating the truths of these foundational principles. Visit awmi.net to get your copy today.

Life Foundations—Live: More of an audio-visual learner? Immerse yourself in these principles with our eight-hour video teaching—recorded live at Charis Bible College—available on the Charis Distance Education platform. https://www.charisbiblecollege .org/distance-education

You might also enjoy these teachings from Andrew Wommack Ministries:

God's Kind of Love: Series available in CD from https://awmi.net or by calling 719-635-1111.

Spirit, Soul, and Body: Teaching available in book form, CD, DVD, and/or as a study guide from https://awmi.net or by calling 719-635-1111.

Identity in Christ and Who We Are in Christ: Available as single CDs from https://awmi.net or by calling 719-635-1111.

The War is Over—God is not mad, so stop struggling with sin and judgment: This teaching on how God sees us is available in book form, CD, DVD, and/or as a study guide from https://awmi.net or by calling 719-635-1111.

The True Nature of God: Available in book form, CD, DVD, and/or as a study guide from https://awmi.net or by calling 719-635-1111.

Believer's Authority—What you didn't learn in church: Teaching available in book form, CD, DVD, and/or as a study guide from https://awmi.net or by calling 719-635-1111.

About the Authors

Husband and wife duo Mike and Carrie Pickett were called to Russia before they met. After having his life transformed by the message of God's love and grace, Mike became an instructor in the school and eventually the director of Andrew Wommack Ministries of Russia. When Carrie graduated from Charis Bible College in 1999, she moved to Russia to plant a Charis Bible College and Andrew Wommack Ministries office. Together Mike and Carrie grew the Russian ministry to reach more than ten Russian-speaking nations.

After sixteen years in Russia, Mike and Carrie relocated to Colorado where Mike now serves as the vice president of Charis Bible College and International Operations of Andrew Wommack Ministries. Carrie now serves as the assistant vice president of Charis Bible College as well as the director of the World Outreach Global Training School at the Charis Woodland Park campus.

They are deeply honored to be part of a ministry that is so active in training and discipling nations. Mike and Carrie have two children, Elliana and Michael—their "missionaries in training."

Fast. Easy.
Convenient.

For the latest Harrison House product information and author news, look no further than your computer. All the details on our powerful, life-changing products are just a click away. New releases, email subscriptions, testimonies, monthly specials—find them all in one place. Visit harrisonhouse.com today!

harrisonhouse.com

The Harrison House Vision

Proclaiming the truth and the power
of the Gospel of Jesus Christ with excellence.
Challenging Christians
to live victoriously,
grow spiritually,
know God intimately.

Connect with us on
![Facebook] Facebook @ HarrisonHousePublishers
and ![Instagram] Instagram @ HarrisonHousePublishing
so you can stay up to date with news
about our books and our authors.

Visit us at **www.harrisonhouse.com**
for a complete product listing as well as
monthly specials for wholesale distribution.